ELDERCARE
CONFIDENTIAL

CAUTIONARY TALES FOR ADULT CAREGIVERS AND CARETAKERS OF PARENTS AND SPOUSES

Chris Cooper

INDIE BOOKS
INTERNATIONAL

ISBN-10: 1-941870-73-2
ISBN-13: 978-1-941870-73-0
Library of Congress Control Number: 2016956030

Designed by Joni McPherson, mcphersongraphics.com

INDIE BOOKS INTERNATIONAL, LLC
2424 VISTA WAY, SUITE 316
OCEANSIDE, CA 92054
www.indiebooksintl.com

CONTENTS

SECTION 1

The Great Eldercare Dilemma

CHAPTER 1

Debunking the Shady Acres Myth

What is the Shady Acres myth? Let's separate fact from fiction.

There is a common misconception of an eldercare Shangri-La, a lovely place to take Mom for her declining golden years. With a little searching, the children or spouse will find a healthy, comfortable, and mostly government-paid-for idyllic home, complete with rocking chairs and lemonade. "Won't Dad just love it here!" All will be taken care of and the children or spouse will be relieved of messy caregiver and caretaker decisions and wrangling.

Caregivers and caretakers faced with challenges of eldercare quickly discover the United States is in crisis. With life expectancy rising and seventy-seven million baby boomers entering retirement age, middle-income American seniors and their family caretakers are facing enormous challenges. They look in vain for their Shady Acres.

Sorry to say, Shady Acres does not exist. Even if it did, you probably could not afford it. Most middle-income Americans are unaware of the crucial fact that the government does not generally cover long-term-care expenses. This can be distressing for the six million Americans age eighty-five and older, a number that will shoot up to more than fourteen million in 2040, according to the U.S. Census.

If a spouse needs long-term care, that is one thing, but if the care is left to one or more of the children, then that can be a sticky situation. There is no simple solution for the sandwich generation that is taking care of children and parents. As writer Jennifer Braunschweiger noted on the More website (http://www.more.com/eldercare): "There's no prenup for eldercare, no contract in which we lay out clearly what tasks we are willing to do, how much time and money we are willing to spend and what responsibilities, if any, lie beyond the scope of the agreement."

Thrust into the Role of Fiduciary

This book is for the caregivers and caretakers who are often thrust into the role of fiduciary, either by legal appointment or by assuming the role because of their relationship to the elderly person who needs caretaking. Typically, this is a close relative, like a parent.

This is a guide to help those facing eldercare issues, such as spending other people's money even if it is on the elderly person, making medical and legal decisions for the elderly person, and the implications of substituted judgement (the standard to be used by surrogate decision makers who have specific knowledge of the elderly person's values and wishes pertaining to health care and other choices).

Eldercare also includes dealing with myriad unexpected problems revolving around money, drugs, and even sex.

All of the fiduciary's actions should be performed for the advantage of the beneficiary. The duties of a fiduciary spelled out by laws include loyalty and reasonable care of the assets within custody. Caregivers and caretakers must not use the assets of the elderly person for their own gain. This is more than a moral responsibility; this is a legal obligation.

Here is a job description for fiduciary: Caregivers need to know about financial matters; have good communication skills and interpersonal skills; possess a great deal of patience and stamina and an understanding of human relations; and acquire a knowledge of health care terms, medical conditions, and medications, because they often need to work through family situations, crises, and life-threatening events related to their elderly person's care, which may also involve dealing with law enforcement officers and attorneys.

According to legal dictionaries, the word "fiduciary" comes from the Latin word *fiducia*, meaning "trust"—a person who has the obligation and power to act for another (often called the beneficiary) under circumstances which require good faith, total trust, and honesty. This trusted care does not come without cost to the caregivers.

Caregiving is not only hard work, it also comes with several financial burdens. These include disruptions to employment, extra costs while caregiving, and even a toll on the health of the caregiver. Here is a look at the three main challenges:

- **Disruptions to Your Employment.** Caregiving takes time. Caregivers often have to use work time to handle caregiving responsibilities. Typically, there will be emergency interruptions that must be dealt with that interfere with work duties. An unexpected fall may require a fast trip to the emergency room. Caregivers naturally find they have to use up their vacation time and sick benefits to provide eldercare. There are other sacrifices, such as giving up advancement opportunities at work and the possible loss of fringe benefits.

- **Tapping into Your Purse and Wallet.** Caregiving takes money. Eldercare is never cheap. Caregivers use more gas and other resources to care for their loved one. There are also costs for delegating tasks a person would have otherwise done for themselves if they had the time, such as lawn care. Additionally, there is the loss of wages or business income and the costs to replace lost fringe benefits.

- **Tolls on Your Health.** Caregiving takes its toll. Not all the costs are financial. Caregiving means increased stress and burnout. The elderly with brain-related issues may exhibit agitation, angry outbursts, or inappropriate behaviors, which might include verbal or physical abuse. Dealing with that can result in spending more on stress relief, such as eating out more often and consuming more alcohol. This gets compounded by the loss of time off and vacation time. There also is the stress of constantly being on vigil (as the Navy would put it, "constantly standing your battle stations"). Often there is increased medical costs for the caregiver from stress related illnesses.

An additional stressor is the proper management of the costs for the care recipient. These include the medical costs not paid for by insurance or Medicare, the legal costs for such things as power of attorney and living trust documents, and the costs of formal caregivers while the caregiver in charge is at work or sleeping. Of course, one of the largest costs for the recipient is the cost of care settings. These include adult day care, nursing homes, and assisted living facilities.

MYTHS ABOUT THE ELDERLY

When it comes to being forced into the role of caregiver, the situation usually begins with a tremendous lack of knowledge. Being unprepared for the role of caregiver is not unusual; people don't know what they don't know. The common hope is that there is an easy solution that others have found. Sadly, this is not the case.

This book aims to quickly bring caregivers up to speed on a number of issues. This Shady Acres eldercare myth needs to be debunked like a lot of other myths about eldercare. Here is a quick sampling of perception and reality.

- **MYTH: Sickly.** Forget the perception that all old people are aging, bedridden seniors who wind up in a nursing home. The elderly are living longer and healthier lives. Studies at Boston Medical Center found that in over 40 percent of seniors who lived to be 100, sickness related to old age did not occur until they were eighty. Census data from 2006 revealed that only 7.4 percent of Americans over the age of seventy-five live in nursing homes.

- **MYTH: Serene.** Many are familiar with the term "the golden years." referring to retirement. Actually, for many these are stressful times. In fact, suicide rates are higher for people over sixty-five than for younger people.

- **MYTH: Senile.** No, not all of the elderly go senile, which actually has come to mean a disease of dementia. In fact, only 8 percent of those over sixty-five will develop some form of dementia, including Alzheimer's Disease.

- **MYTH: Sexless.** Research has found that sexual activity and enjoyment do not decrease with age. As one blogger on certifiedcare.org noted, "some adult caregivers are shocked when a seventy-five-year-old parent who's lost a spouse starts serious dating."

- **MYTH: Surly.** A commonly-held belief is that all old people are surly, irritable, and cranky. As people age, there are more aches, hassles, and challenges that would frustrate anyone. But generally, if people got along well with others when they were young, they will do the same when old. But if someone was difficult to get along with when they were young, they will remain difficult to get along with as they age.

- **MYTH: Strapped.** According to the U.S. Census Bureau, only around 9 percent of Americans sixty-five or older have incomes and assets that fall under the poverty line. Actually, older adults tend to be better about saving money and being careful about their spending. The problems develop when others, like their own children, get control of the money.

But it would be foolhardy to believe that all of the elderly will be able to take care of themselves until they die. Most will need the help of caregivers and caretakers, be that a child or a spouse. That is probably why you are reading this book.

What About Nonmedical Home Care or Continuing Care Retirement Communities?

Some elderly people are hellbent on staying home. This has spawned an entire nonmedical home care industry that is quick to sing the praises of aging in place and not leaving the homestead. Rarely, however, do they discuss the dark side.

If cost savings are the major reason for choosing nonmedical elderly home care, the forgotten expense is senior-proofing the home. Many existing homes are filled with built-in booby traps that become increasingly difficult to navigate with age. Stairs can be a major problem, and while it is possible to install electric chairs on staircases, they are expensive.

There is another problem with the nonmedical part of the caregiving. What happens if Mom keeps pooping her pants? The nonmedical part means in some states the person who comes by is not allowed to touch the elderly person—a fact many caregivers and caretakers do not know until the person is hired and on the job. Also, they definitely cannot give medications.

Some ask: what about continuing-care retirement communities that offer a variety of living options—from independent living to assisted living to nursing care—all within one community? Then Mom or Dad can stay in one place but move from one type of residence to another as their health care needs change.

Sounds good on paper, but they are pricey. Entrance fees for these communities, of which there are some 2,000 nationwide, can run anywhere from $100,000 to $1 million, and monthly fees can range from $3,000 to $5,000, if not more.

Many elderly people overlook the financial risks they take on when signing a contract to move into a continuing care retirement communities. In most states, this is an unregulated industry, and people could lose their entire investment should the community go bankrupt.

THE ANSWER MUST BE ASSISTED LIVING

Ah, some say, Shady Acres does exist: it is called the assisted-living home. They will take care of all the eldercare problems, including those messy drawers. Wrong, wrong, wrong.

Equating assisted-living facilities to an idyllic Shady Acres is a gross miscalculation. Since they came upon the scene in 1981, when assisted-living facilities made their debut as a midpoint between home care and a nursing home, they've steadily grown in popularity. However, these are not charitable nonprofit institutions out to serve the public good; eight out of ten are for-profit, as are about 68 percent of nursing homes. More money at stake can mean more problems.

To be fair, there is no legal definition of assisted-living; this is purely a marketing term. While we know what a nursing home is by law, we cannot be so sure when a facility advertises itself as featuring assisted-living quarters. In fact, we have a much clearer picture of what a hotel is than an assisted-living facility. While I do not have anything against assisted-living facilities making money, people need to know they are not the perfect solution for all. Like any for-profit business, assisted-living facilities are out to make money for their investors. The rising cost of assisted living means that many families need to consider aging in place, home care, and multi-generational housing instead. In addition, just trusting that an assisted-care facility will provide top-notch care is naïve. It is not unusual for an assisted-living facility to begin charging extra fees when a resident's health declines and he needs help with getting dressed, taking medication, or bathing.

On top of that, if the assisted-living facility does not like you, you are out. Residents are asked to leave when they are disagreeable, their health care needs change, or they cannot afford the costs and need to rely on Medicaid. Unlike nursing homes, assisted-living facilities don't have an industrywide process for appealing such decisions when a resident gets a boot out the door.

"We're dealing with an interesting situation," one anonymous caregiver shared about an eldercare eviction. "Our grandpa is in his 80s but he's quite the escape artist and has been escaping care centers for awhile. One time he hacked a keypad and hot-wired a car. He got about twenty-four miles away before we could catch him. Anyway, I understand the 'if we don't like you, you're out' situation. We've constantly had to deal with that with my grandpa the way he is."

So the time has come to put the Shady Acres fantasy to rest once and for all and face reality. The reality is that the elderly and their caregivers and caretakers do not face one solitary problem such as how to find the right care facility. In fact, the problems are six-fold: something I have nicknamed the Six-Headed Eldercare Beast. This is definitely a beast you do not want to face unarmed and uninformed.

ENTER THE SIX-HEADED ELDERCARE BEAST

The dirty little secret of eldercare in America is that it is not just one problem for caregivers and caretakers; instead, it is an interrelated set of a half-dozen problems. All of the problems can come at you at once, which gave rise to the metaphor of a six-headed monster.

When I think of the Six-Headed Eldercare Beast, I am picturing something akin to the multi-headed serpentine monster called the Hydra that Hercules did battle with in Greek mythology. From the murky waters of the swamps near a place called Lerna, the Hydra would rise up and terrorize the countryside. A monstrous serpent with many heads, the Hydra attacked Hercules with poisonous venom.

Like the Hydra of lore, eldercare challenges attack on several fronts. The Six-Headed Eldercare Beast battles caregivers and caretakers with money challenges, medical challenges, psychological challenges, social challenges, environmental challenges, and legal challenges. Some are even a matter of life or death. Making a mistake in any of these six areas can have serious consequences. Part II of this book gives advice on avoiding the following kinds of eldercare mistakes:

- **Money Mistakes.** When it comes to protecting yourself against financial abuse, it's important that you trust your instincts. But there are also practical steps you can take to safeguard your money.

- **Medical Mistakes.** Health care can be an explosive issue that is a chief concern. There are several medical mistakes that can arise in long-term care. It is crucial to keep an eye out for these issues, because they are easy to overlook.

- **Psychological Mistakes.** Unfortunately, many older Americans are living increasingly isolated lives, leading to depression or a general decrease in quality of life. They may be suffering from their own personal neglect, or they may actually be suffering abuse from a neighbor, a family member, friends, or someone else they know.

- **Social Mistakes.** The social area takes into consideration the family (or the lack of family) and the distance the family may live away from the person who needs care. It also involves social situations that can cause clashes because of everyone having an opinion as to what the person's long-term-care needs may be.

- **Environmental Mistakes.** The environmental eldercare concern revolves around where the elderly person lives, or should live. This often creates considerable conflict within the person him- or herself and within the familiy. This is a need that evolves.

- **Legal Mistakes.** In navigating eldercare, few consider the legal aspects. There are many issues that can cause potential pitfalls if not properly documented and understood.

Use This Book as Your Candid Guide

The silver lining on the dark storm clouds of eldercare is that there are information and experts to help guide you. My purpose is not just to raise issues, shatter myths, and point out mistakes. This is not a scholarly textbook or sugar-coated collection of tips. What this book promises caregivers and caretakers is straight talk on the subject.

Providing this information is my life's work. I am the owner and founder of Eldercare Advocates, a private geriatric care management and long-term-care consulting firm. My firm provides comprehensive assessments and planning of long-term-care needs of disabled adults and the frail elderly. Assessments are made across the medical, psychological, social, environmental, legal, and financial aspects of a person's life.

As a professional fiduciary, I work with seniors, disabled persons, and other individuals who can't manage their affairs on their own, assisting with everything from day-to-day financial issues to investment and estate management.

My career began in nursing homes and hospitals. After finishing paramedic training and a degree in nursing, I pursued an interest in how people could finance health care, and primarily acute care. I found out that chronic long-term care is where financial devastation generally occurs for many people, especially the retired.

As an eldercare advocate, it is my mission to educate all involved and provide vital information that is needed to make informed decisions. As the old adage states, "forewarned is forearmed." Before I share some cautionary tales, let me share a confession or two about eldercare.

CHAPTER 2

Confessions of an Eldercare Advocate

Adult children often don't know—or don't want to know—what is really going on with their parents. When a person is thrust into the fiduciary caregiver role, they do not have the luxury of ignorance.

Contrary to the old saying, ignorance is not bliss when it comes to eldercare. Time and again I have seen situations unfold in which it becomes clear that there are many secrets being kept that can have huge impacts on the family. Often, as people get older, they do everything they can to hide the fact that they are suffering from health problems or diminished mental capacity.

One example that comes to mind was a man with an elderly father. The son was a lawyer, but he worked as a litigator and didn't have any expertise in elder law or financial matters. When I met him, his father had recently fallen in the home he shared with his second wife, the son's stepmother. The father had sustained fairly severe injuries and needed to be hospitalized.

Because the second wife had no experience handling finances, she asked the son to step in and figure out where their money was so she could pay the bills. The son quickly discovered that his father had purchased an annuity from an insurance salesman at a local bank. In fact, the father had tied up almost his entire net worth—about $2 million—in annuities.

WHAT IS REALLY GOING ON?

Right away, the son was concerned about the annuities. Since he was a lawyer, he wanted to read all the insurance and annuity contracts and find out what exactly they said. But as he started looking over the documents, he realized that the language was extremely vague and, despite being a lawyer, he was in over his head. That's when he contacted his financial advisor, who brought me into the picture.

When I sat down with the son, the first thing I asked was, "What else do you think is going on?" The son, not surprisingly, said there wasn't anything going on, and that his father and stepmother were doing fine. The house was clean, the car was washed; nothing was wrong. I explained that things might appear to be fine, but that he needed to be careful. Older people often try to hide things from their children, since they don't want the kids to realize they have problems or are disabled.

In this situation, it soon became clear that the father was trying to hide that he was suffering from dementia and that it was no longer safe for him to live in his home. He and his wife had a lovely house in the suburbs, but it was isolated, and they needed help to meet his needs.

Not only was the couple trying to hide their health problems, but the son was also in denial. I had to convince him, using fairly strong language, that his parents were in danger. The father was suffering from dementia and had other health issues, and the stepmother wasn't able to manage things on her own. She couldn't drive or handle many other activities. In addition, it was becoming apparent that she herself also may be in the early stages of Alzheimer's disease. Like many older adults, the couple was doing everything they could to convince other people that there wasn't a problem, like carrying cheat sheets to help them remember the names of family members or keeping things in their pockets to remind them of things. But despite those little compensation methods, it was becoming obvious that there was an issue.

In this situation, it was really difficult to convince the son that he needed to do something. First, he was hesitant to intervene, since he had a busy career and didn't want to become a full-time caregiver (even though he was the only living relative). In addition, the father had inherited some property, which the son expected to receive after the father passed away. I explained to the son that his father might need the money from that property to pay for his care, and that there might not be an inheritance. That made the son *furious*. He didn't understand how this was possible. What he hadn't realized was that the government doesn't pay for nursing home care unless you're broke. Property, if it's not your principal residence, is an asset that has to be spent before you can qualify for public assistance.

After coming to terms with this disappointment, the son eventually agreed that his father and stepmother should move to a private assisted-living community. It's a very nice facility and today the couple is in a much safer environment where there is someone overseeing their care and needs. The son doesn't have to handle day-to-day care and he knows that they're going to be looked after. He has also come to terms with the possibility that they may need to use the property he thought would be his to pay for that care.

MAINTAINING THE FACADE

I hope this story helps you realize that often parents will do everything they can to make sure their children will continue to see them as strong and able to take on the world. They want their kids to think that there will never be a problem and that the parents will take care of everything. In this case, the son was in his fifties and he was just beginning to realize this wasn't true.

Sometimes children do not know the truth about their parents until after they have died. For example, one man had worked for the state government for many years and had seen both the good and bad side of life. After his wife died, his son moved him into an assisted-living facility. While this man was having difficulty living on his own, he didn't really want to move.

This gentleman, who was in his eighties, was a bit lonely in his new home, and as a result, he became friends with several of his caregivers. Two of those caregivers—a housekeeper and a nurse's aide—ended up becoming "special friends," which his family didn't realize until after his death.

After he passed away, the family discovered that the man, who was of modest means, had titled two of his accounts in such a way that he left the money to the housekeeper and the nurse's aide. Upon his death, the accounts passed directly to those women, outside of probate and away from the rest of his assets. When his oldest son found out about what his father had done, he was angry. The younger son was a bit more supportive and loving, perhaps to the point where he was denying that anything had happened. Neither son had known anything about their father's relationship with these two women.

This is not an unusual situation. Often, children don't learn about their parents until after they pass away. That can be a sad thing because the children never really got to know their parents as adults. At the same time, parents often fail to get to know their children as adults. In any case, sometimes we have to understand that parents are just ordinary people with frailties and weaknesses, including loneliness. They have a desire and a need to be with people and around people. Sometimes it's people of the same sex, and sometimes people of the opposite sex. Sometimes it's for sex and sometimes it's just companionship. But whatever it is, we have to learn to accept these things because it's just part of who people are.

The hard part, however, is that sometimes older adults may establish relationships with people who don't have their best interests at heart. Individuals who get involved with an older adult may have ulterior motives, such as financial gain. Sometimes it's an honest exchange, and sometimes it may not be. We can't know the exact situation in the story I just told you. We don't know if there was undue influence, or if the gentleman left the money to the women simply because he cared for them. And his sons will never know because they can't ask him.

But you can ask these questions while your older relatives are still alive, and what's more, you need to. You need to have frank conversations with family members about their lifestyles, goals, and intentions. Sometimes, it may help to have those conversations with your family member in the presence of an attorney, minister, or doctor. The important thing to realize is that these are things that could affect your loved ones later in life, with consequences ranging from sexually transmitted diseases to exploitation and elderly-person abuse.

Coming to terms with the fact that parents are not perfect, but rather are normal, flawed human beings, can be difficult. But accepting this while they are still alive lessens the likelihood of unpleasant surprises after they are gone.

In the next section, I will look at common mistakes that senior-caregivers and -caretakers can make. These cautionary tales will cover the medical, psychological, social, environmental, legal, and financial aspects of eldercare.

SECTION II

What to Beware with Eldercare

CHAPTER 3

The Worst Medical Mistakes

Medicine, thought to be the solution to health challenges in older people, is often the real eldercare problem. What can go wrong? Plenty.

Medical problems are a thorny issue of eldercare that many caretakers and caregivers do not want to acknowledge. But caretakers and caregivers need to face the real medical issues of eldercare.

Some huge challenges include polypharmacy, which is the overtreatment of medical problems with too many medications at once, whether for one condition or many (sometimes obtained from more than one doctor); polymorbidity, which is the simultaneous presence of two or more chronic diseases or conditions in a patient which, when treated improperly, can lead to drug reactions; and those who prey on the elderly with outright quackery, which is the selling of so-called miracle cures and devices for everything from "anti-aging" to heart disease and cancer (a particular pet peeve are worthless copper bracelets promising a cure for arthritis).

Then there are addictive behaviors that may require intervention or rehab center stays. Caregivers need to know that many elderly people abuse drugs to ease their pain. This can happen especially if the elderly person sneaks in substances ("What, my Dad, smoking pot?"), chooses not to take meds as prescribed, or decides to self-medicate with multiple over-the-counter drugs or alcohol.

Bad medicine is costly, both physically and financially. Health care costs can easily spiral out of control. This leads caregivers to look for advice that can be trusted.

So Where are the Specialists to Help?

Caregivers looking for help generally discover it is hard to find. Unfortunately, there is a lack of specialists for the elderly, professionals who are called geriatricians. "Ideally, the U.S. should have one certified geriatrician for every 300 citizens who are 85 or older. In 2013 this ratio is 1:870, and it is going to get a whole lot worse," said Bruce Brittain in "Many Geriatrics, Few Geriatricians," published on ChangingAging.org, February 27, 2013. "Older patients often present symptoms differently, absorb drugs more slowly, respond differently to certain protocols and usually have multiple chronic conditions that overlap. Only a trained eye and mind can deal with these differences."

There is also a dearth of geriatric clinical pharmacology and clinical pharmacy services. According to Daniela Fialova and Graziano Onder in the *British Journal of Clinical Pharmacology* (June 2009), medication use in older adults is often inappropriate and erroneous, partly because of the complexities of prescribing and partly because many patients, providers, and health systems substantially influence the therapeutic value of medications for the elderly.

Often, caregivers seek me out because the medical community doesn't have a cure for what's wrong with the elderly person in their care. The major condition that leads to people seeking long-term-care services is dementia, whether caused by Alzheimer's disease or other diseases.

But there are other reasons for people needing long-term care, including Lou Gehrig's disease, multiple sclerosis, muscular dystrophy, arthritis, hypertension, and strokes, among other things. These are all conditions that can't be cured per se, and therefore, the goal of their care is to stabilize and help them live out their lives more comfortably with all the support they need.

This chapter addresses several medical mistakes that can arise in long-term care. It is crucial to keep an eye out for these issues because they are easy to overlook.

ACCIDENTS AND OVERDOSING ON MEDICATIONS

Not accepting that the elderly person has declined and now requires another level of care can be dangerous. Ignoring the fact that Mom needs a walker can lead to a fall, resulting in broken bones, displaced joints, hospitalizations, and the use of pain medication, which carries its own risks. Leaving Dad unsupervised could lead to accidents in the kitchen and bath, or even a fire. They could cut or burn themselves, leave the stove on, or eat unhealthy foods in excess.

A weekly pill dispenser is a tool, but not a real solution to the dangers of overdosing. There comes a time when the caregiver needs to be in charge of dispensing medication. And there are many other issues when it comes to prescribed medicines.

PRESCRIPTION DRUG CONCERNS

It seems like a fairly straightforward process: when you are sick, you visit a doctor, who prescribes medications to make you well. But what if the medications you're ordered to take are actually having a negative effect on your health? The reality is, some medications are harmful to patients' health—yet licensed physicians prescribe them every day to elderly and disabled individuals.

Medicare Part D provides more than thirty-five million elderly and disabled Americans with critical—sometimes life-sustaining—prescriptions they might not otherwise be able to afford. It's an invaluable program, but as a story by investigative news organization ProPublica revealed, is not without its flaws.

Millions of prescription drugs are dispensed through Medicare Part D, but the program does not regulate the suitability of the medications for individual patients. Instead, decisions about which drugs to prescribe are left to treating physicians, many of whom are overloaded with patients and write an average of 137 prescriptions a day.

As a result, some doctors end up prescribing drugs that are harmful and addictive. In some cases, they just aren't keeping up with research about a drug's approved uses. In others, they may receive perks from pharmaceutical companies in exchange for prescribing certain medications. Some physicians even run drug mills in which medications are indiscriminately dispensed to patients who can pay cash for their visits. As a result, doctors may prescribe drugs in unapproved ways—which can be ineffective at best and deadly at worst.

For example, in 2010 alone, over 500,000 prescriptions were written for carisoprodol, a muscle relaxant also known as Soma, which has been red-flagged by the American Geriatrics Society as a drug elderly people should avoid. Many patients with Alzheimer's were also prescribed quetiapine (Seroquel), an antipsychotic that can increase the risk of death in people with dementia.

Given the lack of government oversight, it's essential for Medicare patients—or the caregivers assisting them—to choose health care providers carefully. Prescriber Checkup (https://projects.propublica.org/

checkup/) is an online tool that allows you to search for individual providers and see which drugs they prescribe.

If you suspect that a loved one is being inappropriately or overmedicated, there are several steps you can take:

- **Keep a documentation log.** Maintain your own records of medications your loved one has been prescribed, including "as-needed" drugs and vitamins. Verify the drugs and dosages with the physicians at each visit.

- **Avoid polypharmia.** It's important to take medications as directed. However, when patients see multiple doctors or use several different pharmacies, they may wind up with more prescriptions than they actually need—an all-too-common condition known as polypharmia. Be sure you understand exactly what drugs your loved one is taking and how they interact with his or her other prescriptions.

If your loved one resides in a nursing home, you can also:

- **Speak to nursing home supervisors.** If you visit your loved one's nursing home to find that they are behaving oddly or seem unusually sedated, speak to the nursing supervisor. Ask for an explanation for any medication or behavioral changes, which should be detailed in the patient's medical chart.

- **Advocate for "redirection."** Redirection is a drug-free method of de-escalation that should be used prior to administering sedation (for example, removing a patient from an agitating situation). Because redirection attempts should be noted in a patient's chart, verify that medication wasn't the medical staff's first course of action in treating your loved one.

The best things you can do to protect the health of your loved ones is to keep detailed records of drugs and dosages, demand explanations for any changes in medications, and talk to a nursing home director or primary care physician if you notice any behavioral changes.

EATING DISORDERS AMONG THE ELDERLY

Eating disorders among the elderly can have many causes. While younger people with anorexia or bulimia often struggle with a distorted body image, the underlying issues may be somewhat different in older adults. Changes in taste or smell, other psychological conditions (like depression), cognitive problems, the death of a loved one (especially someone with whom the person shared meals), loneliness, and a desire to regain a sense of control (especially among people who are living in nursing homes) can all contribute to eating disorders in elderly people. In severe cases, refusing to eat may be a form of "silent suicide." Elderly women are more likely than elderly men to suffer from an eating disorder, but the condition occurs in people of both genders.

Frequently, eating disorders in elderly patients are not recognized either by health care providers or a patient's family. People may simply not notice the person's weight loss, may assume that weight loss is related to other health issues, or that it is a natural consequence of aging. Of course, an older person's weight loss is not always due to an eating disorder. Poverty (not being able to afford food), limited mobility (not being able to get to the store to purchase food), medication side effects, or a related medical condition can all cause weight loss in older adults. Once you've realized that an older person is losing weight, determining the exact cause is important, since this will dictate how the problem is treated. Identifying and managing an eating disorder is especially important, since weight loss can seriously compromise a person's health, especially if they have other health conditions. In serious cases, an eating disorder can cause death.

If a doctor or another health care professional has determined that an elderly person is suffering from an eating disorder, proper treatment and management of the disease is essential. Usually, it is best to treat whatever underlying issue is triggering refusal to eat (such as depression related to the loss of a loved one). Becoming aggressive or hostile or attempting to force-feed a person will often not have the intended effect, and may even make the condition worse. Being supportive and understanding will typically lead to more success, especially if it's coupled with the support of a health care professional who has experience treating eating disorders in elderly patients.

Some specific strategies that may help an elderly person with an eating disorder include:

- Lifting dietary restrictions on consumption of high-fat or high-salt food

- Adjusting the person's diet so that they are served more of the foods they like

- Serving the person several small meals throughout the day, rather than just a few big meals

- Using additives to improve the smell, appearance, or taste of food, especially if the person has lost some of the sense of smell or taste

- Encouraging the person to socialize and be active, including eating with others

- Making sure the person participates in rehab or other activities to build strength and endurance

Patience and compassion are key when dealing with an older adult with an eating disorder. Working closely with the individual's medical team will also be helpful in creating a plan that allows the person with an eating disorder to improve their health. The important thing is to realize that eating disorders are not a normal part of the aging process, and that they can have serious health consequences. Fortunately, eating disorders in older adults can be treated, improving a person's health and hopefully allowing them to live a longer life.

CHAPTER 4

The Worst Psychological Mistakes

First, let's address the psychological elephant in the room for caregivers: the child now has to take care of the parent.

Mentally, that is an enormous challenge. Even in the best of parent-child relationships this shift of power is difficult; when the relationship is unpleasant, it makes it extremely hard.

A psychological defense mechanism that typically occurs is denial. Often, the caregiver will go into denial and refuse to make tough decisions that need to be made. They do not see that no decision is actually a decision, and often not the best one for the elderly person under their care.

One book I recommend for caregivers is *A Gradual Disappearance* by Elizabeth Lonseth, which was described by aplaceformom.com as "a warm, personal and concise guide for people who have a loved one with Alzheimer's disease or dementia." In her book and speeches, Lonseth cites several problems that denial can lead to and raises important issues:

- **Competency and Capacity.** One problem stemming from denial, says Lonseth, is not getting needed legal papers in place, such as financial power of attorney, medical power of attorney (also known as advance health directive), and written permission for adult children to see their health records. Without those documents in place, getting proper care, dealing with finances, and authorizing needed medical procedures can be difficult. The caregiver would have to go to court to get legal rights to supervise the elderly person's care, in the form of a conservancy (or guardianship), which is expensive to initiate and maintain—not to mention the time it would take. Obtaining a conservancy also involves having the elderly person be deemed incompetent, which can be very humiliating for them. Once they are deemed incompetent, they can no longer execute legal documents.

- **Financial Exploitation and Black Sheep.** When a caregiver is in denial about a parent's memory loss, the elderly person is vulnerable to financial exploitation. Taking away checkbooks and control of finances is extremely difficult; but to not do it allows others, including family members, to exploit the elderly person. A prime culprit is a child, maybe a black sheep of the family with a problem such as drugs or gambling, who sees nothing wrong with taking advantage of the parent. Some even reason, "This money will be coming to me when they pass on, but I need it now."

- **Sibling Reactions and Family Conflict.** "Denial on the part of a family member can cause major family conflict," says Lonseth. Those in denial create all kinds of frustration for those who are the caregivers facing the disease. She adds: "The children in denial don't help out and the aware ones take on multiple burdens, sometimes alone. Often the ones in denial accuse their siblings of overreacting. The ones in denial don't think additional care is needed and Mom or Dad can be retrained to make their own meals or dress themselves."

DEPRESSION AND THE ELDERLY

First the good news: Americans are living longer, more independent lives. According to the Department of Health and Human Services report, *A Profile of Older Americans: 2012*, the number of Americans over age sixty-five increased from 35 million in 2000 to approximately 41.4 million in 2011. That is an increase of 18 percent in just ten years. The same study estimates that by 2040, the population of older Americans will nearly double, reaching 79.7 million.

Now the bad news: Unfortunately, many older Americans are living increasingly isolated lives, leading to depression or a general decrease in quality of life. It is estimated that 46 percent of women seventy-five and older live alone. Even more disturbingly, the highest suicide rate in the United States is among white men aged eighty-five and older, according to the National Institute of Mental Health's 2015 report, *Older Adults and Depression.*

Depression in the elderly can cause dementia-like symptoms. In the psychological area, many people are concerned when their family member is depressed or confused. They are concerned that the person may not be doing what they need to be doing to take care of themselves. Thus, they may be suffering from their own personal neglect, or they may actually be suffering abuse from a neighbor, a family member, friends, or someone else they know. Any of these areas can be difficult, because the psychological realm is often the most difficult area to recognize and treat; the symptoms are likely not physical. There are also limited cures or treatments for these problems.

While many are aware of the common signs of depression (for example, sadness, loss of interest, and social withdrawal), initial signs may be subtle or difficult to identify. Often, depression in older people can manifest as an increased fixation on aches and pains. Yes, it is true that as you get older, your body breaks down some; however, concern or complaining about small aches and pains shouldn't dominate one's life.

Similarly, a sudden lack of motivation or energy may be a reason for concern. Elderly people shouldn't expect to feel like they did in their twenties, but a significant drop in energy that cannot be attributed to an injury or other medical condition may be early warning signs of depression.

Coping with a loved one who is aging can be challenging. Those challenges are often magnified when your loved one is suffering from depression, which is frequently stigmatized and misunderstood. Even friends or relatives who want to provide support may not know the best way to help. While every situation is different, below are five strategies that you can use if you're trying to help a loved one with depression:

- **Get Educated:** Taking steps to educate yourself about your loved one's illness is one of the most important things you can do. Understanding their symptoms, treatments, and recovery plan will make it easier for you to support your friend or relative. Education can also reduce stigma and help you understand sometimes troubling symptoms. Being familiar with your loved one's illness can also prevent you from offering unhelpful or judgmental advice (for example, telling a person with depression to "just cheer up" or "look on the bright side").

- **Get Support:** Having a loved one with depression can be stressful and disruptive. Taking advantage of support services can help you connect with others who are in a similar situation and increase your knowledge. The National Alliance on Mental Illness (NAMI), for example, offers a wide variety of support groups and resources, both for people with mental illness and their loved ones. Connecting with these resources can help you decrease feelings of isolation and manage your own emotions regarding your loved one's illness (which will make it easier for you to help them). In some cases, you may want to seek support from a therapist, psychiatrist, or psychologist yourself.

- **Don't Blame Yourself:** It's possible you are wondering if you are somehow to blame for your loved one's depression. Or perhaps you feel ashamed or guilty about not recognizing someone's symptoms sooner or doing more to help. Remember, the causes of depression are complex, and trying to assign blame is not likely to be a helpful exercise at this point in time. Instead of dwelling on what could have been, look for ways that you can help your loved one in the present.

- **Allow Your Loved One Independence:** People with depression need to be treated with respect. Resist the urge to exert too much control over your loved one's life, since one major challenge for people with depression is the feeling that they have lost control. Rather than making assumptions about what would be best for your loved one, talk to them about what kind of support they want and need on their road to recovery. An open discussion may yield some surprising information.

- **Maintain a Positive Attitude:** Conveying an attitude of hope can be an important part of your loved one's dealing with the issue. You can also acknowledge the courage your loved one displays in seeking treatment, which is often an extremely challenging thing to do. Compassion and acceptance can be extremely valuable to those who have depression.

PSYCHOLOGICAL ISSUES OF CAREGIVERS

A caregiver should not be in denial about his or her own signs of stress and psychological strain, which can often be brought on by the mental and physical exertions of caregiving. Don't neglect your own health, both physical and mental. Taking care of yourself will allow you to take care of those who are closest to you.

So what can you do if you appear to be showing early signs of psychological stress and strain? Take action with the following steps:

- **See your doctor.** The first step you should take if you are concerned about stress and depression is to talk to your doctor. As a society, we have gained a greater appreciation for mental health issues, yet we often resist seeking help for ourselves.

- **Get some exercise.** The last thing you might feel you want to do is get outside and move, but it really is a good step to take. Many studies have shown that the impact of regular physical exercise can be equal to or greater than that of prescription medication. Try a walk around your neighborhood; you'll get some good exercise, and it can help you connect with your community.

- **Connect with friends and family.** Spend time with those you love. Reach out to people you may not have seen in a while. When we are working, we are often too busy to make the time for friends.

- **Embrace Your Life.** By staying active and engaged with family and friends, you will improve both your physical and mental health—allowing you to get the most out of your golden years.

Dealing with Transfer Trauma

Transfer trauma, also known as relocation stress syndrome, refers to the negative effects that elderly people can endure when moving to a new home. Although transfer trauma affects people of all ages, it's a serious concern for the elderly; they can suffer severe physical and psychological symptoms. Those who are struggling with cognitive impairment, such as seniors relocating to an assisted living facility, are even more likely to exhibit symptoms. It's important to learn about the causes and risks of transfer trauma so that you and your loved ones are better able to prevent it.

Recent research has evaluated the trauma endured when elderly patients are forced to relocate. Transfer trauma has been found among the elderly when they move from their homes to a long-term-care facility and even when they relocate within a facility.

Common symptoms include fatigue, insomnia, anxiety, depression, and a sense of being lost. Seniors who are suffering from mental impairment, such as patients with dementia or Alzheimer's disease, seem more prone to serious symptoms. For such patients, the feelings of loneliness, confusion, and sadness that stem from being disoriented in a new environment are more likely to be exacerbated.

Left untreated, relocation stress can lead to long-term debilitating effects, and it can take a significant toll on a senior's body. Studies indicate that the mortality rate of patients with relocation stress can triple if not addressed by their caretakers. A senior's ability to function may permanently decrease, demonstrating why such trauma must be addressed by competent mental health professionals.

Research into elderly-person transfer trauma indicates that risks are involved with any major move late in life. Certain situations are more danger prone than others, however, and they are proportionate to the gravity of the move. For example, elderly patients who move from their homes to a residential facility will be more vulnerable than those who switch rooms within the same nursing home.

Relocation can be especially difficult for patients who don't understand why the move is necessary and believe that they are capable of living independently. This is why patients with Alzheimer's disease are significantly more vulnerable, since their memory loss can inhibit their ability to understand why they have moved.

While certain populations are more susceptible, it's critical for seniors and their loved ones to understand that relocation stress syndrome can affect anyone. Since symptoms may not clearly point to transfer trauma, it's imperative that the syndrome stays on the radar of family members with loved ones moving into a facility.

The primary means of preventing elderly-person trauma relates to the most common cause of the suffering: the loss of control over one's life. Once the root of the trauma has been addressed, patients have shown the ability to move homes considerably more smoothly. In this regard, the most essential preventive measure is involving seniors in the decision-making process as much as possible.

If seniors are not able to actively participate, then it's important that their loved ones remain attentive to their concerns. Being an active listener and answering questions can be a tremendous help in preventing or alleviating the confusion that can come with moving homes.

It's also helpful to be with seniors while they are acclimating to their new environment. The presence of familiar faces can help the elderly adjust to their new homes and reduce the likelihood of harmful stress. In the next chapter, we'll look at the social aspects of eldercare.

CHAPTER 5

The Worst Social Mistakes

The Dutch have a saying: "The world is good, but the people could be better." Some people can be true allies in providing eldercare. Others can be your worst enemies.

When it comes to eldercare, there are good things to be said for the interaction with others. Sadly, there is much bad be said about social interactions too.

Social mistakes take into consideration the family (or the lack of family) and the distance the family may live away from the person who needs care. They can also involve the elderly person's neighbors and neighborhood, social events (such as their lodge, church, synagogue, and other places like that), their culture, and their upbringing.

BE ON THE WATCH FOR BLACK SHEEP

Many caretakers and caregivers thrust into eldercare are looking for all the help they can get, especially if the elderly person is suffering from short-term memory loss, bad driving habits, and accidents around the house. But beware of relatives who are wolves in sheep's clothing.

"You may have just discovered that the black sheep of the family—the unemployed nephew, the ex-doper niece, the eternally lazy long-lost son or grandson—has just moved in (perhaps with a few of his equally shifty pals), offering to take care of an elderly in-law in exchange for free rent, use of the car or to watch out and protect them as they grow older," says Leslie Albrecht in a 2008 *Law Officer* magazine article.

Shady characters are not just relatives, either. Sometimes the abuser is a neighbor who has volunteered to help look after the elderly person in need of care. "Even a supposedly reputable caregiver company may have installed what looks like a crook to provide health care, companionship, or to watch over your relative," writes Albrecht.

Quite quickly, cash, jewelry, and other pawnable

items go missing. The caregiver needs to step in before this all-too-common elderly person abuse scenario plays out.

BEWARE DANGEROUS AND HARMFUL RELIGIOUS GROUPS

Religion is always a touchy subject. Many religious organizations provide comfort and fellowship for the elderly. A caregiver might not agree with their religious views, but those views should be respected.

However, even mainstream religious organizations can unknowingly cause problems. I know of one elderly woman who was a devout Catholic. Based on her donations, she was soon on many legitimate Catholic charity mailing lists. As the mailings came in, she would dutifully write a check to each organization, thereby overdrawing her checking account every month until the caregiver was able to step in and take her checkbook away.

One person's worthy religion might be called a cult by another; however, the caregiver cannot be in denial that there are dangerous and harmful religious groups that prey on the elderly for their own ends.

Some religious groups and charismatic televangelists can exert undue influence on elderly persons. These religious organizations send out volumes of letters urging elderly to join and "set the example for youth" or to help "the less fortunate in the world."

Abuse can run deeper than just overzealous fundraising. Religious group observers have heard many stories of groups even bilking seniors out of food stamps and social security payments. More affluent elderly all over the world are urged to turn over homes and property, or to sell them and donate the profits to the group. One religious group allegedly forces elderly persons to donate money and sign deeds for the church's "visionary projects."

There are horror stories about the elderly who went to live in religious group homes who have had to turn over all assets and then went hungry, living in squalid, crowded conditions, and received no medical care. Some were made to work by the religious group. Officials, however, were told the elderly were only pursuing hobbies. Thus, they could continue to receive their social security checks.

Stay on Guard for Alcohol Abuse Enablers

Alcohol abuse can be a problem for those needing eldercare. A caregiver should not assume that a social organization is benign. Some local social organizations—such as fraternal lodges like the Elks, Eagles, Masons, Knights of Columbus and Veterans of Foreign Wars—can just amount to nothing more than drinking clubs that are cheaper than bars.

There is another potential alcohol problem to be addressed: alcohol abuse by the caregiver. Some researchers say little attention has been paid to the relationship between caregiver burden and alcohol use. Caregivers who experience social and emotional burden related to caregiving are also at risk for problematic alcohol use.

Little wonder. Caregivers tend to report worse physical health, including insomnia, headaches, and weight loss and are more likely than noncaregivers to put off seeking needed medical care. Caregivers also report higher rates of depression and anxiety than noncaregivers. Additionally, caregivers tend to report poorer quality of life than noncaregivers.

If you see this problem in a social club or another caregiver, or you see it in yourself, then you need to do something about it.

Be On the Lookout for Sex for Favors

Adult children taking care of elderly parents need to take the blinders off when it comes to sex. Children need to learn to see parents as adults—adults with needs and desires.

I know of a nurse's aide who was paid $500 to work naked in an elderly man's house. One shocked son told me this tale about his widowed father. Although the parents had created a will and trust to pass assets along to their children when they died, Dad never bothered to retitle the assets to the trust when Mom passed away. When Dad moved into a senior housing complex, he began making deals for sexual favors with a nineteen-year-old housekeeper. When the father passed, it was discovered he had brought in a bank officer to guarantee his signature on an account that legally passed $300,000 to the housekeeper.

Beware the Abused Caring for Abusive Parents

Many children were abused while growing up. Under the stress of eldercare, might these abused become the abusers, torturing their abusive parents as a method of coping?

The Senate Special Committee on Aging estimates as many as five million elderly Americans are abused each year. According to the National Center on Elder Abuse, abuse falls into the following categories:

- **Abandonment.** The desertion of a vulnerable elderly person by anyone who has assumed the responsibility for care or custody of that person.

- **Emotional abuse.** Inflicting mental pain, anguish or distress on an elderly person through verbal or nonverbal acts.

- **Exploitation.** Illegal taking, misuse or concealment of funds, property or assets of a vulnerable elderly person.

- **Neglect.** Refusal or failure by those responsible to provide food, shelter, health care or protection for a vulnerable elderly person.

- **Physical.** Inflicting, or threatening to inflict, physical pain or injury on a vulnerable elderly person, or depriving them of a basic need.

- **Sexual abuse.** Nonconsensual sexual contact of any kind.

Research reveals those who report having endured childhood maltreatment are more vulnerable than other caregivers to depression when tending to their abusive parents, according to *The New York Times* in a Jan. 20, 2014 article by Paula Span, "A Risk in Caring for Abusive Parents."

This finding emerged from a study by two Boston College researchers, using 2003 to 2005 data from a continuing survey in Wisconsin. The researchers located 1,001 adults over age 65 who were caring for one parent (generally a mother) or both. Almost 19 percent reported physical, verbal or sexual abuse as children, and 9.4 percent reported neglect. The researchers divided their sample into three categories: those with no history of childhood abuse or neglect; those who had been abused and were caring for their non-abusive parent; and those who had been abused and were, to borrow the study's memorable title, "caring for my abuser." They also compared caregivers neglected as children with those who were not neglected. Those who had been abused or neglected were more likely to have symptoms of depression—like lack of appetite, insomnia, trouble concentrating, sadness and lethargy—than those who had not been. No surprise there, perhaps. But the link was strongest for the third category. "The key was caring for the abusive parent," said the lead author, Jooyoung Kong, a doctoral candidate in social work. *Years later, "they are still affected. They're more depressed."*

Span noted the study does indicate that caregivers with a history of maltreatment should be aware of the risk they are taking. If the strain of caregiving becomes overwhelming, there is an increased risk the child who is now the adult caregiver will abuse the elderly parent, "perpetuating a sorrowful cycle."

This cycle of abuse is not limited to children now caring for parents. Many workers in the helping trades were also abused as children. Under the stress of caregiving, antisocial behavior can raise its ugly head. Siblings, friends, and caregiver supervisors cannot close their eyes to this possibility.

CHAPTER 6

The Worst Environmental Mistakes

When it comes to eldercare, there is no such thing as being safe at home. The home environment is full of risk. Selecting the right environment for the elderly person to live in is a series of tough decisions that the caretaker and caregiver must negotiate.

As Nancy Kriseman said in her book, *The Mindful Caregiver*, "Caregiving will never be one-size-fits-all." This is especially true when it comes to choosing the right environment for the elderly person.

Questions abound: What is the right environment? Should they stay in their house, apartment, or condo? Does the home have stairs? What is the accessibility for walkers and wheelchairs? How secure is the place where they will live? What is the neighborhood like these days? Is safety a concern? What transportation is available? Do they need skilled medical care? What level of skilled care is needed?

And of course the big question: How much does it all cost and can we afford it?

Determining the answers often creates a great deal of emotional conflict within the elderly person themselves and within their families. Discussions typically begin around the topic of whether they should live in their own home or a congregated setting with other elderly persons.

Is Staying at Home a Viable Choice?

Several factors come into play when evaluating the safety of an elderly person remaining in his or her own home. Is the home isolated from city services, fire departments, medical facilities, and retail stores? Sometimes it occurs that the surrounding environment may be changing. The neighborhood may be deteriorating. Crime may be increasing. There may be drugs and other problems in the neighborhood that people are not seeing or are choosing not to see.

Additionally, many little things inside the home can make a big difference in how someone gets along from day to day. Sometimes, small changes can help prevent big problems. Let's talk safety hazards. Things like loose rugs and lack of good lighting can be extremely hazardous to someone with impaired sight or mobility problems. They are simple things to correct and will make a world of difference.

As people age, they may be less agile and not able to step over loose rugs. Take a look at the floor surface under those throw rugs; it may be slick or carpeted with a heavy shag that makes getting around difficult. If the lighting is poor, it compounds the danger of slipping and falling because of the floor coverings.

Are electrical outlets plentiful enough to avoid too many extension cords? If not, are the extension cords lying out in the walking path through the house? This is important to look out for. They not only pose a trip hazard, but can also be the source of an electrical fire if overloaded, frayed, or run under rugs.

What kinds of difficulties is the elderly person having in getting around the house because of stairs, or cooking because a stroke has left them with a weaker arm? Looking at how someone goes about their day-to-day life can yield ideas for simple adaptations of equipment and could help someone stay in their home a little longer. For example, steps into the house may impair an elderly person's ability to get out to go shopping, run errands, and socialize with friends. This loss of mobility can impact the senior's social life and therefore increase isolation and depression.

For an elderly person who spends most of the day in one area of the house, check to see that they can get to the bathroom and prepare lunch on their own. If an emergency were to arise, could an elderly person who has difficulty walking or who uses a wheelchair get out of the house by themselves? Are the heating and cooling systems sufficient to meet their needs? If a house is too cold, a furnace check might be in order, or perhaps an update in the insulation in the attic. Consider general maintenance of the house. Is there anything that is jeopardizing the safety or functional ability of an elderly person?

Don't forget to look at the outside of a home. Is parking adequate and nearby? Are the sidewalk and entrance leading to the front door in good shape?

Knowing what a person's environment is like can help in making major decisions. The condition or accessibility of a house could be the deciding factor in whether someone decides to stay in the home or move.

If you have a loved one—perhaps a parent or another elderly relative—who is no longer able to live safely on their own, you may be looking into the possibility of moving them to a nursing home. But nursing homes aren't all created equal. While cost is certainly a concern, you also need to look at factors, such as a facility's environment, the type of medical care provided, and even the quality of food that's served.

Many things can cause clashes during a time of disability—everyone has an opinion about what the elderly person's long-term-care needs may be. This is a good time to have family meetings, because there will be conflict and you must all work together to make important decisions. Clear communication is vital to creating a successful elderly-person care plan.

COMMUNICATION IS ALWAYS KEY

As we reviewed in Chapter 2, many aging family members are actively trying to downplay or disguise their changing needs. Many are reluctant to discuss health issues with family or ask for help. While it could be uncomfortable to have frank conversations, everyone will be better off in the long run if the lines of communication are open.

It is common for problems to arise when some of the following issues are not properly discussed:

- **Medications:** Which medications are they taking? Are they following the instructions and keeping track of them and their interactions?

- **Physical Symptoms:** Are they having difficulty with mobility, urination, sexual activity? Are there new or worsening symptoms that they do not want to bring up?

- **Doctors:** Are they confused about instructions from their physician? Are they resisting prescribed medications or devices such as canes, walkers, hearing aids, or glasses?

While this may be uncomfortable at first, frequent communication with your elderly loved one is essential to their care. Make sure you are kept in the loop about doctors' appointments, medications, and other care recommendations. Offer to help organize information or pills in easier ways to alleviate any confusion they are feeling. Remind them that while certain changes may be unpleasant, they will help maintain their mobility and keep a better quality-of-life for longer. Be sure these conversations are not interrogations, but encouraging exchanges to help them navigate these changes.

One situation that many children of aging parents dread is taking away the car keys. In American culture, driving often equals independence, be it logistically or psychologically. If vision, hearing, and coordination are impaired beyond a certain point, allowing the elderly family member to continue driving could lead to disaster. Reticence to take a sense of independence away from a parent can lead to delaying it long past the point that it is safe.

When the time comes to make this change, communication is again extremely important. You should explain clearly that this is in the person's own best interest and that they could be putting many people at risk by not giving it up. To alleviate concerns over being stuck in the house or unable to do things they enjoy, make a firm plan for when you or someone else will take them to participate in those activities or take care of errands or appointments.

Dealing with Sibling Eldercare Housing Disputes

While the image of a happy family where everyone always gets along is pleasant, this simply doesn't represent reality for many people. Take the story of a brother and sister that I knew. As children, these two siblings had never really gotten along, and as adults, they'd become estranged. Eventually, however, it became clear that they were going to have to come together to deal with the needs of their elderly mother, who had severe dementia and could no longer live independently. Unfortunately, each sibling had different ideas about the kind of care she really needed.

The sister had found a family home where she thought her Mom could live. It was a small place with just six beds. A couple ran the facility, and there were no nurses or other medical professionals on staff. The home only cost $1,000 a month, which was a big plus in the mind of the sister. However, when the brother came into town to deal with this issue, he had a different idea about what would be best for the mother.

This visit was the first time he'd seen his mother in many years, but he realized right away that something was definitely not right. Even though he wasn't that involved in the family, he saw that his sister's idea wasn't the best. That's when he called me to set up a meeting with him and his sister to talk about how to care for their mother.

When I sat down with the two of them, it was obvious that they were very estranged. However, they were cordial and civil to each other and to me. The siblings told their mother's story, explaining that she had become very dependent and was having a lot of trouble remembering to do things on her own. In addition, she was a diabetic and needed a daily insulin injection. Of course, this family home the sister had found didn't have any medical staff, so it wasn't at all clear how the mother was going to get the care she needed if she moved there. In fact, when the brother went to visit the family home and asked how this situation would be handled, he got a very telling answer. The man who owned the home said, "Don't worry, she'll get her insulin every day." *Wink, wink.*

That response was a huge red flag. What the home's owner meant was that an untrained, unlicensed individual was going to be giving the mother her insulin injections. Obviously, that wasn't an acceptable situation. Unfortunately, the mother was at the point where she couldn't afford anything other than this basic level of care. The only other option was a nursing home, since that's what Medicaid would pay for. And that's exactly what the sister wanted to avoid. However, I explained to the brother and the sister that the nursing home was the preferable option, because their mother simply wouldn't be safe in the family home setting because of her medical issues.

Since then, the siblings' Mom has passed away. She ended up living out the rest of her life in a nursing home, where she had very good care and actually improved from living on her own. She was eating better and getting her insulin on a regular basis, and there was always someone paying attention to her needs. In the end, the siblings made the right choice.

The dilemma this brother and sister faced isn't uncommon. Often, when adult children try to make housing arrangements for parents as they become disabled, they don't consider the right factors. They may not like the idea of a nursing home. They may think certain facilities are too expensive. There can be a temptation to go for the cheapest option possible. Well, just as there's a big difference between the cheapest hotel and the most expensive hotel, there's a huge variation in the level of care you get at a basic family home versus a nursing home. If your elderly parent needs medical care or supervision, a nursing home may be the best—and safest—option. And in this case, that's what the brother and sister hadn't seen right away—that their mother's medical needs outweighed some of their other concerns.

This was also a situation in which the sibling's estrangement could have caused real problems for their mother. Fortunately, the brother and sister, despite their personal conflict, were able to sit down and come to an agreement without having to resort to more formal mediation or litigation, and without the state needing to come in and appoint a guardian. This is a good story to keep in mind when you're making your own decisions about caring for an elderly parent since it's an excellent example of the importance of dealing with disputes about care before they become big problems that end up causing harm to the very person you're trying to help.

THE APPEAL OF SHARED HOUSING WITH ROOMMATES

Less-than-optimal finances and a desire for companionship have inspired some older adults to make a lifestyle choice more often associated with college kids and recent grads—they're taking on roommates.

An article in *InvestmentNews* (August 18, 2013), "Meet the Real Golden Girls," profiled a handful of Baby Boomer women who are turning to shared housing in retirement. Could cooperative housing be the future of retirement in America?

For many elderly, shared housing can be appealing for a number of reasons. Reducing expenses is certainly a primary motivation for those who choose to live with people other than a spouse, partner, or children as they age. Combining households can be a way to make rent, mortgage, and utilities more affordable. It can also allow people to live in an otherwise unaffordable neighborhood or in a larger house rather than a smaller apartment or condo. These financial benefits are especially important for older single women, who often have limited financial resources (in fact, a study from Demos.org found that nearly half of women over age sixty-five face serious economic insecurity).

But shared or cooperative housing has an appeal that goes far beyond financial factors. With rising rates of "silver divorce" (divorce later in life), many middle-aged and older women are finding themselves living on their own. While some welcome the privacy and solitude of solo living, others want the social life and friendship that comes with living with other people. Shared housing arrangements are especially popular among women, who tend to live longer than men, and are more likely to be single (44 percent of women older than sixty-five are single, compared to less than 25 percent of men older than sixty-five).

THE COST OF NONMEDICAL IN-HOME CARE

If the shared housing is not an option for your elderly family member, but they are not yet ready to be moved to a care facility, you should do what you can to ensure they are not overly isolated.

Lack of interaction can lead to depression and, some experts argue, even a decline in physical health. If you or other family members and friends cannot afford the time to take care of the elderly person, there are alternatives.

Whether the elderly person lives with you or on their own, they could benefit from someone checking in on them on a consistent schedule. A visiting hired caregiver can help with a variety of chores and errands, from cleaning and grocery shopping to picking up medications and preparing nutritious meals.

Nonmedical home care services provide regular visitation and can even evaluate environmental issues in the home (which were discussed in the previous chapter). This type of arrangement could alleviate stress over a lack of visitation.

If the elderly person prefers being at home, the cost of additional care might be worth it. While more long-term-care insurance companies are paying for nonmedical home care, it's primarily paid for by the family or the seniors themselves. While costs are different in each state, prices run between $10 and $30 per hour, according to Carol Marak on the Home Health Care Agencies website, homehealthcareagencies.com/.

Not everyone requires full-time care. Marak estimates that 22 percent of their eldercare clients employ hired caregiver services four hours or less per week, and 20 percent use them between four and eight hours per week.

While a part-time hired caregiver might be a good solution, typically there does come a time that the elderly person needs to have both nonmedical and home health care services at the same time. That's because a licensed medical professional who administers home health care is different from the services given by a nonmedical hired caregiver. Marak explains the difference:

> Home health care is typically chosen when a person leaves a hospital, skilled nursing facility or rehabilitation after an inpatient stay. Home health care benefits seniors with medication changes in need of monitoring and education on potential side effects. For example, it works best for individuals with decline in physical functioning by offering physical and/ or occupational therapy in-home to assist in

regaining independence. Home care is best for individuals needing some help with activities of daily living like meal preparation, cleaning house and laundry. Transportation to and from doctor appointments, shopping, and errands. It's available short-term and used after a hospital stay resulting in limited mobility. In this case, recovering from surgery, one needs both home health and in-home care services.

While both focus on safety and well-being, the hired caregiver establishes and maintains a personal relationship with the elderly person and provides the amount of time that might not be practical from a family member like a son or daughter with their own career and family responsibilities. But when the elderly person is recovering at home from a stroke or surgery, then a licensed medical professional is needed until their condition improves.

WHAT WILL MEDICARE PAY FOR?

Medicare, as well as private insurance, will pay for some services, like visits by nurses, and speech and occupational therapists. When a patient is discharged from the hospital, Medicare will pay for a nurse, occupational and speech therapist for the senior at home, but only according to a doctor's prescribed plan of care.

According to the 2011 MetLife Market Survey, a home health agency is likely to employ a range of medical professionals. The types of positions include physicians, registered nurses, licensed practical nurses, physical therapists, social workers, speech-language pathologists, occupational therapists and certified aides.

In March of 2014, the New York Times reported that Medicare officials updated the agency's policy manual—the rule book for everything Medicare does—to erase any notion that improvement is necessary to receive coverage for skilled care. Unlike the past, Medicare now pays for eldercare nursing care, physical therapy, and other services for beneficiaries with chronic conditions like Parkinson's or Alzheimer's disease. The change affects care from skilled professionals and home health and nursing home care, for patients in both traditional Medicare and private Medicare Advantage plans.

But there are times when staying at home is not the answer. Two other options to consider are assisted living communities and residential care homes.

Assisted Living Communities and Residential Care Homes

Assisted living communities are similar to retirement communities, but they also have on-staff caregivers. These caregivers can provide assistance with a number of daily activities from housekeeping to taking medications. Assisted living communities often consist of private apartments and are ideal for elderly persons who could use assistance with basic care needs, but who don't require constant medical attention.

Assisted living facilities (ALFs) go by many names: domiciliary care facilities, personal care homes, residential care facilities, adult congregate housing, community residences, and sheltered care facilities. Assisted living, by any name, provides care for elders who need help with daily activities but want to retain as much independence as possible. Most facilities offer 24-hour supervision and an array of supportive services with more privacy, space, and dignity than many nursing homes, and at a lower cost.

Assisted living facilities offer a middle-ground between independent living and nursing home care.

These homes follow a philosophy of personalized care that allows a resident as much autonomy as s/he wants or needs. Assisted living facilities attract people who require help with activities of daily living but do not need the skilled medical care provided in a nursing home. Residents can choose the level of care they require and define their own lifestyle needs. Most facilities provide housing and personalized support services to meet the daily needs of residents. The staff of ALFs generally encourage the involvement of residents and their families, neighbors, and friends in planning programs and creating a supportive environment. The advantage of assisted living is that elders can receive substantial care in a more residential (and less restrictive) environment than a nursing home or long-term-care facility. Since the 1980s, thousands of assisted living facilities have sprung up in response to the need for a place where elderly and disabled people can receive care, but retain their independence. Residences might be provided in a large house in a community, in a newly built free-standing structure, or in connection with independent apartments or a nursing home.

Although services vary greatly, residents typically enjoy their own room or apartment, three meals per day, assistance with personal care, laundry service, transportation and medical supervision. Some facilities also arrange for residents to receive senior services in the community, such as adult day care, transportation, and recreation. Facilities may also include these elements:

- Safety features, such as grab bars and wheelchair ramps

- Social work assistance to coordinate services

- Health and exercise programs

- Nurse or a medical clinic in the building

- Housekeeping and laundry

- Community areas for social activities

- Security and emergency call systems

Residents or their families generally pay the cost of care for ALFs because few subsidies are available. In some cases, health insurance or long-term-care insurance may reimburse certain costs of the facility. Some state and local governments offer subsidies for low-income elders in ALFs. Depending on state regulations, your elder may be eligible for Supplemental Security Income (SSI) or Medicaid payments.

Experts expect more states to begin offering benefits to pay for assisted living homes because they are less costly than long-term care and serve the needs of elders who want more independence. ALFs are owned and operated by both for-profit and nonprofit organizations and can range in cost from $800 to $3,000 a month. Fees may be inclusive, or there may be additional charges for special services. Costs are generally lower than home health services or nursing homes.

The typical resident is seventy-five years or older, female, and widowed or single. However, residents may be young or old, affluent or low-income, frail or disabled. Older residents come to assisted living facilities from nursing homes, hospitals, or their own homes or apartments. Many older people, with a wide range of conditions, continue to live in assisted living programs even when they become more disabled. The number of residents living in a facility can range from several to 300 persons, with the most common size from twenty-five to 120 individuals.

NINE NURSING HOME SELECTION TIPS

Below are a few nursing home issues to keep in mind as you tour different facilities and make a choice about where the elderly person under your care should live.

Here are some tips to guide you in evaluating potential nursing homes.

- **The best time to tour a nursing home is on a
  Saturday evening.** Because administrative and
  marketing staff won't be around at that time, you'll
  get a truer picture of what life is really like at the
  facility.

- **Make sure you visit when a meal is being served.**
  You'll get a chance to see the quality (and quantity)
  of food firsthand. Make sure every resident gets
  enough to eat and that staff are available to help
  those who need assistance.

- **Find out how often the nursing home brings in
  nurses from a staffing agency.** It's not unusual
  or a bad thing for a nursing home to occasionally
  have to turn to an agency to shore up its staff—
  after all, you want an adequate number of medical
  personnel on hand at all times. But if the nursing
  home is always bringing in new staff who aren't
  familiar with the facility or the patients, that could
  result in a lower quality of care for your loved one.

- **Consider long-term care.** Medicare offers very
  limited coverage for nursing home stays. That's
  why many people purchase long-term-care

insurance or set aside money so they can pay for care out of their own pocket.

- **Consistency of caregivers matters.** In some facilities, a patient's caregivers may change from day to day. That can be unsettling and confusing for patients. Try to find a nursing home where the same caregiver sees the patient on most days.

- **You need to be proactive to make sure your loved one gets the care they need.** Often, it helps to designate a single family member to serve as the representative who will take charge of the patient's care and deal with the nursing home.

- **Your loved one probably won't be able to choose their doctor.** Instead, they'll be limited to whatever doctor(s) work with the nursing home. The facility's doctor may also be responsible for numerous patients. Nursing home doctors may visit the facility just once a week to make quick visits with patients.

- **You should make your family member's room feel as much like home as possible.** Bring personal objects and pictures so the place is familiar and comforting to them.

- **Theft can be a problem.** If your loved one has valuable items (like jewelry) make sure that they aren't left out anywhere where they could easily disappear. If possible, mark valuable items with your loved one's name.

PAYING FOR NURSING HOME CARE

According to the National Institute on Aging, it's important to check with Medicare, Medicaid, and any private insurance provider you have to find out their current rules about covering the costs of long-term care. You can pay for nursing home care in several ways. Here are some examples:

- **Medicare.** For someone who needs special care, Medicare, a Federal program, will cover part of the cost in a skilled nursing home approved by Medicare. Check with Medicare for details.

- **Medicaid.** Medicaid is a State/Federal program that provides health benefits to some people with low incomes. Contact your county family services department to see if you qualify.

- **Private pay.** Some people pay for long-term care with their own savings for as long as possible. When that is no longer possible, they may apply for help from Medicaid. If you think you may need to apply for Medicaid at some point, make sure the nursing home you're interested in accepts Medicaid payments. Not all do.

- **Long-term-care insurance.** Some people buy private long-term-care insurance. It can pay part of the costs for a nursing home or other long-term care for the length of time stated in your policy. This type of insurance is sold by many different companies and benefits vary widely. Look carefully at several policies before making a choice.

When thinking about nursing home costs, keep in mind that you can have extra out-of-pocket charges for some supplies or personal care—for instance, hair appointments, laundry, and services that are outside routine care. The rules about programs and benefits for nursing homes can change. Visit www.medicare. gov for information about different care options. To learn more about the Medicaid program, see www. medicaid.gov.

CHAPTER 7

The Worst Legal Mistakes

I n my opinion, the hardest-to-find competent professional to find in most of the United States is an elder law attorney. In navigating eldercare, many miss the critically important legal aspects. There are many issues that can cause potential pitfalls if not properly documented and understood. Here are just some of the hidden trap legal issues that are a part of eldercare:

- Consenting to medical treatment

- Consenting to nonmedical services, such as counseling

- Consenting to release of confidential information

- Determining and monitoring residence

- Protecting property and assets

- Obtaining property appraisals

- Receiving income for the estate

- Making appropriate disbursements

- Serving as a guardian

- Obtaining proper approval prior to selling any asset

- Reporting to the court on estate status

- Making end-of-life decisions

None of these can be handled without the proper legal documents. The only thing worse than not having these documents is having the wrong documents.

NAVIGATING THE LEGAL MINE FIELDS

Caregivers thrust into the eldercare fiduciary role need to get up to speed on the difficult legal decisions that need to be made. Handling legal care issues is like learning to walk through a minefield. This is no time to rely on trial and error. To learn to walk through a minefield, you would find a trusted advisor who knows how to do it, so that he or she could give you a map and teach you the way through.

Unfortunately, in the minefields of eldercare, the right advisors and the maps are hard to find. Elderly people are often victimized by trusted advisors and family members by the very legal documents and title forms they provide. Again, it is very difficult to find a competent elder law attorney in the United States. But find help you must to obtain the right durable power of attorney, a will or living trust, and a health care directive while the elderly person is still of sound mind.

If the elderly person still has the capacity to deal with their financial, legal and health care affairs, then legal planning for eldercare should begin as soon as possible. Putting this off (or if it was put off) can cause a world of hurt.

Planning should be put in place with all due haste. Here are the basics to give you a quick overview:

- **Last Wills and Living Trusts:** Thanks to countless movie and television plots, most people are aware that a will is a legal document that specifies what should be done with someone's assets and belongings when they die. A last will also names the executor—a trusted person who is charged with handling the wishes of the deceased. To be effective, the will must be determined to be valid and genuine, which is the role of probate court. People often set up living trusts to avoid the probate process, which takes time and can be costly. Unlike a will, a court of law typically does not need to validate a living trust. In a living trust, a person's assets are transferred to the trust, and that person can name others to be in charge of the trust when he or she becomes incapacitated or dies. State law will dictate what is to be done with a person's assets if they die without a will or living trust.

- **Durable Power of Attorney.** Do you need a power of attorney (POA) in place? No, you need a durable power of attorney in place (DPOA), and here is why. The creator of a POA, called a principal, grants another person, called an attorney-in-fact, legal rights to act on the principal's behalf. However, the moment the principal became incapacitated, the POA would be terminated and the attorney-in-fact would have no legal rights. Additionally, the disabled principal would then need a guardian. Simple POAs are rarely used today. To overcome limitations of the POA, state legislatures created the DPOA, which remains in effect after a principal becomes incapacitated. Under a DPOA, a principal names an attorney-in-fact (sometimes called an agent) who will manage all the principal's affairs after the principal becomes incapacitated.

- **Living Will or Health Care Directive.** What if the elderly person becomes incapacitated, terminally ill, or is unable to communicate his or her wishes? That is when a living will—also known as health care directive or advanced directive—is useful. Many consider it also important to file a legal document called a Durable Power of Attorney for Health Care (DPOAHC), which names a person as a health care agent. This agent has the authority to make necessary health care decisions and is responsible for ensuring that providers carry out the wishes of the incapacitated person.

- **Guardianships and Conservatorships.** As a last resort, guardianships and conservatorships may be the only way to ensure that the personal and financial affairs of an elderly person are protected. According to the National Guardianship Association, fully two-thirds of guardianships in America are family guardianships. A judge will appoint a local professional guardian if relatives are far away or if the family dynamics are difficult. There are no national guidelines for guardians, and most states do not offer guidance for this important role. Be aware that guardianships and conservatorships are more expensive than routine legal planning because of the necessity of court involvement. Guardianship proceedings are also inherently adversarial, and a contested case can be difficult for a family to overcome. Guardianship will typically last as long as the need arises. By far, most last for the remainder of the elderly person's life. In a guardianship proceeding, a court decides whether the elderly person has diminished mental capacity and should not retain the rights to make decisions. Often. a concerned family member or friend of the elderly person consults an attorney, who gives guidance on obtaining medical evidence from physician, psychologist, or psychiatrist examinations. Once the evidence is gathered, a petition that states why guardianship is necessary is filed with the court. The court will ultimately decide if the elderly person needs a guardian.

The Advantages of a Durable Power of Attorney

The primary functions covered by a DPOA—and thus the key reasons why you should establish one—are health care and finances. Creating a DPOA for health care will give a designated person the authority to make medical decisions on behalf of the principal while a DPOA for finances will allow the designee to handle legal and economic affairs.

Any power of attorney ceases to operate once the principal dies. However, it's while the principal is living that there is a distinction between the two forms of legal documents. A regular power of attorney is effective only when the principal has the legal capacity to act. When he or she is injured, sick, or disabled to the point of being unable to communicate, the agent's authority ends. The durable power of attorney remains in effect even if the principal becomes incapacitated, making it a highly important estate planning tool.

Consider this: if you were to become debilitated or incompetent without preparing a durable POA, your family and friends would not be allowed to maintain your financial affairs or make important health care decisions on your behalf. (Or let's say it was your elderly parent who is the incapacitated one; you would be unable to make any decisions on their behalf, including crucial Medicaid planning.) Anyone who was hoping to serve as the elderly person's agent and undertake these tasks would have to go through the expensive and often contentious process of Probate Court and be officially appointed as guardian.

Instead of naming one DPOA to cover all contingencies, a person can create a separate Durable Power of Attorney for Healthcare (DPOAHC) or Durable Power of Attorney for Finances (DPOAF). The DPOAHC is limited to making health-related decisions for the principal while a DPOAF only oversees financial matters for the principal.

FINANCIAL INSTITUTIONS REFUSAL OF POWERS OF ATTORNEY

Financial institutions, for their part, have started rejecting financial maneuvers made under the cloak of a power of attorney, for fear of being parties to fraud or elder abuse. "Even with perfectly executed power-of-attorney documents, it's still hard to get banks to honor them because they are concerned about their own liability," reported Kelly Greene and Jessica Silver-Greenberg in The Wall Street Journal (May 14, 2011).

Not long ago, power-of-attorney documents were rarely challenged or exploited. But Green and Silver-Greenberg report that prosecutors and elder law attorneys say "the number of cases of adult children purloining assets from parents' accounts is rising. That is prompting lawmakers to turn their attention to power-of-attorney abuse—often the first step in a swindle."

The same article cited that MetLife Mature Market Institute, a research unit of insurer MetLife Inc., placed annual financial loss suffered by victims of elderly person financial abuse, including exploitation of powers of attorney, at $2.6 billion back in 2009. That same year, philanthropist Brooke Astor's son grabbed headlines when he was convicted of grand larceny, among other counts, for using a power of attorney to increase his own salary, ultimately siphoning more than $1 million from her.

Banks and brokerages, meanwhile, are taking matters into their own hands, imposing tough new hurdles on power-of-attorney claims, "making it much tougher for well-meaning adult children to take the reins when their parents' health falters."

THE DIFFERENCE BETWEEN A POWER OF ATTORNEY AND A TRUSTEE

Attorney Brenda Geiger, of the Geiger Law Office of Carlsbad, California, says many people she advises are confused by the difference between a power of attorney agent and trustee. Here is how she explains the difference.

A trustee is the person or entity that protects and manages the assets in a trust. For a revocable living trust, the trustee is usually the person who created the trust. The trust document will have a successor trustee or set of successor trustees. The successor trustee usually takes power when the person who created the trust either becomes incapacitated or has died. The trustee only manages assets that are owned by the trust, not assets outside the trust. Common assets that are owned by a trust include things like real estate, bank accounts, nonretirement brokerage accounts, LLC interests, stocks, corporate interests, and personal property. Trusts can also own other types of assets, such as cars, boats, annuities, intellectual property, or even a note or partnership interest.

If the asset is owned by the trust, then the trustee holds title to that asset. The trustee can typically borrow, sell, encumber and invest in these types of assets (if the trust document gives them the power to do so). Things that cannot be owned by a trust typically include retirement accounts and sometimes life insurance. There are special types of trusts that can own insurance. Most revocable living trusts, however, are not of that species of trust.

In contrast, a Power of Attorney does not own

anything that is owned by your trust. The Power of Attorney controls assets that are not inside your trust, such as retirement accounts, life insurance, sometimes annuities, or even bank accounts that are not in trust title. A Power of Attorney agent (if granted authority) can also have power over your tax return filings. If granted authority, your Power of Attorney agent can also disclaim property left to you, or even apply for governmental benefits on your behalf. A Power of Attorney may also be given authority to create further trusts for you for estate planning purposes.

CUSTOMIZE THE DOCUMENT FOR YOUR NEEDS

Like a trust, a durable POA can be written so that the transfer of responsibilities occurs as soon as the document is executed. This type of POA is known as immediate. The other option is to state that the POA goes into effect at the time when a specific event— such as the disability of the principal—occurs. This kind of POA is referred to as "springing."

Either of these options can be written in several ways, to encompass whatever scope of authority the principal desires their agent to be responsible for. You can choose whether your document says that the POA has the authority only to pay bills or sell certain assets. Or you can decide that POA extends to complete financial decision-making, from managing all assets to selling the family home to dealing with the IRS.

THINK AHEAD AND PLAN

You need to be proactive. The time to prepare this legal document is before one starts having trouble handling certain aspects of life. At the time a durable POA is signed, the principal must be capable of deciding to seek assistance. Thus, anyone who is in advanced stages of Alzheimer's disease would most likely not be considered "of sound mind" and therefore legally unable to appoint a POA.

Considering your own competency and decision-making abilities can be difficult. No one wants to face the fact that a time might come—or perhaps may already have arrived—when such responsibilities may be beyond your capabilities. In addition to the fear of losing independence, it's not uncommon to worry about whether the person you choose to handle your affairs will somehow go against your wishes.

That's why it's essential to start the discussion early— while your family member is in good mental and physical health, and there is time before the need for an agent should arise—about who would be the ideal candidate to serve as the designee and how wide the scope of their responsibilities would be.

And don't worry about making a decision now that will last forever, without any change or flexibility. The signed document can be revised or revoked at any time, as long as the person is considered competent (otherwise, it stays in effect until death).

Preparing a durable POA for both health care and finances is an essential part of financial planning. Having these documents in place will ensure that your family member's wishes for medical treatment and monetary matters will stay in the hands of trusted people that they have chosen.

EVICTION FROM A NURSING HOME

Here is another example of a legal problem that might occur. Because the demand for nursing home beds can outstrip supply, facilities may try to evict residents they deem difficult. Eviction is only allowed for six reasons:

- Failure to pay

- A resident no longer needs nursing home care

- A resident's needs cannot be met in a nursing home

- A resident is endangering others' safety

- A resident is endangering others' health

- The facility is going out of business

The facility must give written notice of the eviction to the resident, usually within thirty days of the discharge, and provide facts supporting it. The notice must include telephone numbers of the nursing home inspection and licensing authorities and instructions about how to appeal.

Source: E. Carlson, "20 Common Nursing Home Problems and the Laws to Resolve Them," *Clearinghouse Review Journal of Poverty Law and Policy*, January/February 2006, quoted by Deborah Lorber in The Commonwealth Fund.

CHAPTER 8

The Worst Financial Mistakes

I n the financial area, most people seek out financial planners when faced with long-term care of a family member. They want to know "Can we afford to pay for this?" and "Can we get out of paying for this?"

Unfortunately, the answer to either question is unknown, because long-term care can last a long time. That's why we call it long-term care. It's not short-term, like when the elderly person is in the hospital. Therefore, many people will have conflicts in this area. They are given bad or conflicting advice from attorneys and others regarding these issues. Ideally, caretakers and caregivers need an objective, independent third party who can give the advice needed when faced with this part of long-term care.

Professionals in my arena are just the sort to give you that unbiased advice.

THE ETHICS OF MEDICAID PLANNING

Medicaid planning is a controversial issue. Medicaid is a federal program that targets the poor. When the time comes for paying for your long-term-care needs, an elderly person may end up spending their savings and then relying on Medicaid for assistance. That's because due to the lack of any other program, Medicaid has, by default, become the long-term-care insurance of the middle class.

With the help of attorneys, some elderly people needing long-term care artificially impoverish themselves in order to qualify and preserve their savings, either for their healthy spouse or their children. Some argue it's highly unethical to transfer funds to family members simply so that the government will foot the bill.

Here are some facts to consider. Medicaid typically pays for a semi-private room in a nursing home, but not all nursing homes take Medicaid. In many states, it is not easy to get Medicaid to cover home care or pay for assisted living. Many elderly people want to stay at home, but with Medicaid, they may not be able to.

Medicaid provides health coverage to approximately 72 million Americans, including eligible low-income adults, children, pregnant women, elderly adults and people with disabilities. Medicaid is administered by states, according to federal requirements. The program is funded jointly by states and the federal government.

Many states have expanded coverage as part of the Affordable Care Act ("Obamacare"), particularly for children, above the federal minimums. For many eligibility groups, income is calculated in relation to a percentage of the Federal Poverty Level (FPL). For example, 100 percent of the FPL for a family of four was $23,550 in 2013. The Federal Poverty Level is updated annually. For other groups, income standards are based on income or other nonfinancial criteria standards for other programs, such as the Supplemental Security Income (SSI) program.

What is ethical, unethical, and just plain illegal when it comes to Medicaid planning? The Centers for Medicare and Medicaid Services (CMS) is committed to combating Medicaid fraud, waste, and abuse which diverts dollars that could otherwise be spent to safeguard the health and welfare of bona fide Medicaid enrollees. CMS also has broad responsibilities under the Medicaid Integrity Program to provide effective support and assistance to states in their efforts to combat Medicaid fraud and abuse and to eliminate and recover improper payments.

MEDICARE VERSUS MEDICAID

Unlike Medicaid, there are no income limits restricting people from joining Medicare. The key to maximizing Medicare is understanding the system and the options it presents. Mess this up and it will cost you.

Medicare is not forgiving. Elderly people who don't act during the initial enrollment period find themselves without health insurance for a significant length of time.

Medicare can leave eldercare caretakers and caregivers confused about the choices, and it is only getting more complex. Caregivers need to keep abreast of continual changes in coverage, reimbursement rates, and the revolving Medicare-endorsed private managed care plans, called Medicare Advantage, available in their area.

Simply put, Medicare is health insurance for the elderly. This federal program, administered by the Centers for Medicare & Medicaid Services

(CMS), has a network of nearly 778,000 health-care professionals and more than 6,000 hospitals across the United States.

The Original Medicare Plan is a fee-for-service program that's made up of two components: Medicare Part A and Part B. Medicare Part A is hospital insurance, which covers everything from general hospital stays to rehabilitation in a nursing home for acute illnesses.

Medicare Part B is basic medical insurance that covers services ranging from doctors' visits and outpatient hospital care to physical and occupational therapy and even some home health care

Should a person miss his or her six-month enrollment window, the wait to enroll for Medicare Part B could be long (until the following enrollment period—January 1 through March 31 of the following year) Enrollment in Part A is usually automatic. Coverage would then begin the following July.

WHAT THE AFFORDABLE CARE ACT MEANS FOR EARLY RETIREES

Prior to the passing of health care reform, early retirees who no longer received health insurance from their past employers struggled to find affordable health insurance. It was not unusual for people who fell into this gap to go without insurance until they became eligible for Medicare coverage at age 65.

The Affordable Care Act ("Obamacare") has brought about major changes in America's health insurance system. Early retirees may benefit from a greater choice of plans, more affordable premiums and increased stability in coverage. More people can now consider early retirement as a viable possibility. But before you say "goodbye" to your employer, you should familiarize yourself with how the ACA works.

As a result of the ACA, health insurers can no longer deny you coverage based on preexisting conditions. What previously had been the greatest difficulty for early retirees—securing adequate health coverage with a preexisting condition—has now become a relatively seamless process. Considering that early retirees may have chronic diseases—high blood pressure, diabetes, etc.—that can be extremely costly without health insurance, this reform is a major game-changer for millions of Americans approaching retirement. These people no longer have to factor preexisting conditions into their retirement calculations, which is a tremendous relief for those in their late 50s and early 60s.

Another key advantage for early retirees is that the ACA limits the amount that health insurance companies can increase your premiums based on age. Previously, older Americans were commonly charged premiums that were exponentially more expensive than for those in their 20s and 30s. Limits on age-based premium increases have the potential to save early retirees a significant amount of money. Premiums for older individuals have now been capped at three times the rates offered to younger Americans.

Early retirees may qualify for tax credits when buying health insurance on the state-run health insurance exchanges.

In addition to the aforementioned benefits, some early retirees will qualify for tax subsidies when they purchase a health insurance plan from their state's exchange or on Healthcare.gov. The tax credits apply if you are earning between 100 percent and 400 percent of the poverty line, unless your state has not expanded Medicaid, in which case the first benchmark is set at 138 percent. To give you an idea of what these numbers mean, the 400 percent benchmark includes individuals earning less than $45,690, couples earning less than $62,040, and families of four earning less than $94,200 in income.

Early retirees should take note of the fact that eligibility for tax credits is based on income, not assets. For example, if the bulk of your assets are in tax-deferred retirement accounts, such as an IRA or 401(k), then you may qualify for a tax credit, even if your savings are substantial. Similarly, if you withdraw money from a Roth IRA or Roth 401(k), that sum will not affect your tax credit eligibility, since it has already been taxed.

In addition to your income, the size of your tax credit is related to your age—the older you are, the larger the subsidy for which you are eligible.

CALIFORNIA AND MEDI-CAL

California is just one of fifty states in the union: it is, however, the most populous state and deserves some special attention. Approximately more than eight million Californians receive coverage through Medi-Cal. In addition, with expanded eligibility guidelines related to the rollout of the ACA, approximately 1.4 million more residents may now be able to join the program.

Medi-Cal is the state of California's health insurance program for low-income residents. The program, which is the state's version of the federal Medicaid program, provides coverage for people whose incomes are less than 138% of the federal poverty level.

Do I Qualify for Medi-Cal?

As part of health care reform, the Medi-Cal enrollment process has been simplified for many people. Covered California, the state's health insurance marketplace, acts as a one-stop-shop for people applying for health insurance. (Visit www.CoveredCA.com or call 800-300-1506 to apply.) You have to provide some basic information, which will be used to determine which program you are eligible for (such as Medi-Cal or a subsidized policy you buy through the health insurance marketplace) and sign you up for coverage. In addition, people can continue to apply and enroll in Medi-Cal through traditional channels.

Medi-Cal Coverage

Simplified enrollment through Covered California should make the process of getting Medi-Cal coverage easier for many people. But here are some tips to help you successfully apply for Medi-Cal, especially if you are applying via mail or through your local county social services department.

- Apply as soon as you think you are eligible: Medi-Cal may be retroactive up to three months.

- Use a current address: You'll want to respond promptly to any Medi-Cal notices you receive, so it's important to use a mailing address that is checked daily.

- When submitting information by mail, get documentation: Medi-Cal correspondence may be lost or ignored. Keep track of your submissions by mailing everything via Certified Mail, Return Receipt Requested.

- Respond to requests for information quickly: If Medi-Cal requests additional information from you, provide it as quickly as possible, because this will speed up the processing of your case.

- Appeal: If your case is denied, you can appeal. Working informally with your local office could also help you get the mistake corrected, but filing a formal appeal may ultimately be more effective.

- Beware of estate recovery: In some cases, the estate of the Medi-Cal recipient will have to pay back the program after the recipient's death.

- Don't assume you don't qualify: If you or a loved one is in need of health coverage, don't assume that you don't qualify for Medi-Cal because you have too many assets. The eligibility rules are fairly generous, with many assets considered exempt. You can visit www.CoveredCA.com to see if you're eligible, or visit your local social services office.

For people with low incomes, Medi-Cal may be an affordable path to health care coverage. And with recent changes, enrolling in Medi-Cal should be easier than ever. Following the above tips should help simplify the application process and make it easier for you or a loved one to get coverage.

ELDER FINANCIAL ABUSE

Elder financial abuse or exploitation are the terms used to refer to a wide range of situations where a senior's financial resources are exploited for the benefit of the perpetrator. Many seniors are susceptible to elder financial abuse because the perpetrators are likely to be their family members or caretakers. This means that the stakes are high and that most instances of financial abuse go unreported—according to National Adult Protective Services Association (NAPSA), only one in forty-four cases is reported to the authorities.

Here are the most common examples of such crimes:

- Stealing a senior's money or property, directly or through misusing a joint bank account

- Abusing power of attorney, such as persuading a senior to sign over control of their finances against their interests

- Offering care and companionship in return for money, and abandoning the senior upon receiving compensation

- Pressuring a senior into agreeing to an ill-advised loan without intending to pay it back

- Threatening to neglect the senior's needs unless exorbitant sums of money are paid

- Refusing medical treatment on behalf of the senior so that the perpetrator can use the funds for their own interests

- Forging a senior's signature on a contract or other financial document

- Investment schemes in which unrealistic claims are made to the senior, e.g., pyramid schemes

According to NAPSA, the overwhelming majority of perpetrators—a whopping 90 percent—are individuals whom the victim trusts. They might be family members, neighbors, caretakers, attorneys, or financial advisors. Many times the offender is in desperate need of cash due to personal problems including substance abuse, alcoholism, gambling debts, or other financial woes.

In a minority of cases, the perpetrators are con artists who pose as caretakers until they've earned the trust of the senior. Once the victim has grown dependent on their care, they then exploit the senior for their own monetary benefit.

The statistics indicate that all elderly Americans should be concerned with elderly-person financial abuse, but certain seniors are particularly prone to being exploited:

- Seniors who are cognitively or physically impaired

- Seniors who are dependent on others to help them with their day-to-day needs

- Seniors who are financially naive or ignorant of their personal finances

- Seniors who are suffering from social isolation and loneliness

- Seniors who have recently lost a portion of their retirement savings

If you or a loved one is a senior experiencing any of the following, then it may be an indication that you are a victim of financial abuse:

- Transactions on bank statements that you cannot explain

- Missing money, possessions, or important financial documents

- Bills and statements no longer being mailed to your residence

- A loved one, caretaker, or other professional behaving in a suspicious manner with regard to your finances

- You've signed contracts or agreed to financial arrangements that you do not understand

Protecting Against Elderly Person Financial Abuse

When it comes to protecting yourself against financial abuse, it's important that you trust your instincts. But there are also practical steps you can take to safeguard your money:

- **Monitor joint accounts:** All joint accounts bring along financial risks. Do not create a joint account with someone you do not trust, and keep vigilant tabs on any joint accounts to make sure funds are not being misappropriated.

- **Maintain financial records:** It's helpful to have documentation of all of your financial dealings. Do not pay a bill, lend money, or sign a financial document without recording all of the key details.

- **Keep an eye on your finances:** Don't allow yourself to be in a position in which you're unaware of your finances. Being ignorant of your assets and investments will make you an easy victim for a potential offender.

- **Safeguard your financial information:** By protecting sensitive financial documentation from the eyes of others, you'll make it much harder for a perpetrator to gain access to your assets.

- Learn about your finances: Ask questions if there is anything that you don't understand about a financial dealing.

- Enduring power of attorney: If you are unable to manage your own finances, protect your financial interests by giving over the authority to someone you trust on your own terms (as discussed in the previous chapter).

If you suspect you or someone you know is the victim of financial abuse, you should also contact the authorities, including the police and state or federal regulatory agencies. Watching out for suspicious activity and taking corrective action as soon as you notice a problem can help to mitigate the damage of elderly-person financial abuse.

FINANCIAL FRAUD AND ABUSE

Financial fraud and abuse can happen to anyone, but older adults are particularly vulnerable. Unethical individuals may prey on older adults who aren't as savvy as younger consumers, or who may have mental impairments that make it difficult for them to make financial decisions. Often, these individuals are targets because they've worked hard for years and accumulated significant wealth.

The Certified Financial Planner Board of Standards (the group in charge of licensing Certified Financial Planner [CFP] professionals) recently put together a guide, "Financial Self-Defense for Seniors," designed to help seniors protect themselves from unscrupulous financial professionals. Here are a few red flags the guide suggests watching out for, either for yourself or when advising an older loved one:

• **The advisor has a lot of useless designations or credentials.** Virtually anyone can call themselves a financial planner or financial advisor. Many of these people will have fancy-sounding credentials following their name. Some credentials (like Certified Financial Planner professional, or Chartered Financial Analyst) are legitimate, and a sign the advisor has extensive training and expertise. Others are basically meaningless and require little special study or training. Research an advisor's designations. You should also ask what organizations supervise the advisor (such as FINRA, the Financial Industry Regulatory Authority, or the SEC, the Securities Exchange Commission) and then check with those groups to see if there has been any disciplinary action against the advisor.

- **You're confused about the product you're being sold.** If you don't understand what kind of financial product you're being sold, don't buy it. Make sure you understand the risks, benefits and costs of any product. For example, complicated products, like variable annuities, may be sold to seniors who don't completely understand the fine print, such as high annual expenses and costly withdrawal fees. If you have concerns or a product seems especially complex, don't hesitate to get a second opinion from another financial professional.

- **You're offered "free" advice that's actually a sales pitch.** Older adults often receive invitations to free dinners and seminars on financial education. There's nothing wrong with attending these events. But be aware that the presenter's ultimate goal may be to sell you a particular product or service. If you attend such an event, don't take the advice offered there at face value. If the offer is intriguing, research it on your own, and then contact the advisor if you're interested in pursuing it further.

- **Offers that sound too good to be true.** Whether it's a great deal on a new car or an investment that promises a truly amazing return, if an offer sounds too good to be true, it probably is. Remember, all investments come with risk. Be extremely skeptical of anyone who promises you a "guaranteed" or "safe" return. Regulated brokers and advisors aren't permitted to make such claims.

- **Friends, family members, or acquaintances who are offering financial advice.** Unfortunately, financial scams and abuse sometimes start close to home. There have been cases of religious leaders selling inappropriate products to their congregants, for example, or of community leaders using their respected position to abuse people's trust. Even if you know someone personally, be sure to do due diligence before taking their financial advice. Ask the same questions that you would of any financial advisor: Are they a fiduciary? How is he or she licensed or supervised? What is his or her experience? If anything seems amiss, walk away, no matter how much you like the person. A true friend will not pressure you to make financial decisions that aren't right for you or that you're not comfortable with.

- **The advisor offers to complete the paperwork for you.** Always complete all financial paperwork yourself. Sign documents personally, and don't leave blank spaces that could be filled out by someone else later. In the best-case scenario, the person completing the paperwork could make an innocent but serious mistake. In the worst case, he or she could deliberately falsify information with the aim of defrauding you.

Don't let yourself or a loved one become a victim. Familiarize yourself with common red flags so that you are prepared to avoid financial abuse.

SECTION III

Eldercare That Works for All

CHAPTER 9

Concerns About Long-Term-Care Insurance

There are many myths and misunderstandings about long-term-care insurance. This is by far the youngest form of insurance in the market, and therefore, companies that offer it do not really know if the cost models are accurate. About ten percent of the people I advise have it, which is high compared to the industry average. However, I have to warn them that this does not solve all of their problems. This in no way insures their entire total need.

Some people believe Medicare covers long-term eldercare; as discussed in chapter 8, however, the federal program covers only short stays in skilled nursing homes or a limited amount of at-home care, and it has strict conditions on that care. The joint federal–state Medicaid program does provide for long-term care, but you would need to meet low-income and asset requirements.

There's no question that long-term-care insurance is valuable—after all, according to the Centers for Medicare and Medicaid Services, 70 percent of people over the age of 65 will need some degree of care.

Without insurance, the unexpected costs of in-home assistance or nursing home residency can take a huge bite out of your retirement savings. While prudent, however, purchasing a long-term-care insurance policy doesn't always mean you're financially set in case of illness. The long-term-care insurance industry is facing an increasing number of changes—and that means, so are policyholders.

A BRIEF TROUBLED HISTORY OF LONG-TERM CARE

Horror stories of elderly people not being able to get the care they need have made headlines. The following cautionary advice is excerpted courtesy of law.freeadvice.com.

While nursing homes have been around for many years, the concepts of "at-home" care and "adult day" care were foreign to most people. However, as longevity rates increased due to new medical technologies and drugs, more and more people were living longer than expected. Those that needed some type of long-term care were fairly limited in their options.

During the 1980s, additional options for long-term care started to emerge. Assisted living communities became more popular and many found themselves on long waiting lists because there simply weren't enough facilities to meet the demand. Eventually, more were created and the concept changed a bit. Facilities started offering graduated care —something that made real sense. A person could live in a facility and receive varied degrees of care. If, and when, that person needed more care, he could simply add on additional services for an additional fee. Nursing homes saw the value in that concept and many simply converted a wing of their facility to accommodate those people who only needed occasional services and offered them the option to "move down the hall" when they needed more care.

Unfortunately, traditional health insurance generally didn't cover these types of expenses and long-term-care insurance was still in its infancy. The result was that many people had to sell their homes in order to pay for full-time care before state aid would kick in. At the same time, home care and adult day care eventually started to become more popular and more and more insurers saw the need for long-term-care insurance. By the late 1980s and early 1990s, long-term-care insurance was a hot commodity. Everyone had to have it and insurers made a pretty penny on the deal.

GOOD POLICIES GONE BAD

Problems began to arise a few years ago as policyholders, who had been making premium payments for years, started seeking their policy benefits. What insurance underwriters didn't know at the time was how much health care costs would rise over the next twenty years and how much longer Americans would live. Suddenly, insurers realized that they had underestimated their exposure. While some stepped up to the plate and made good on claims, more did not. Horror stories of elderly people not being able to get the care they needed started to make the headlines. Insurers were, and still are, being accused of simply ignoring policyholders and hoping they would die before any proceeds would have to be disbursed.

The issue has now become both litigious and political. Policyholders have begun suing their carriers for failing to pay for legitimate claims. The lawsuits have made national headlines and have gotten the attention of politicians, so much so that Congress and the General Accounting Office are investigating certain insurers over their marketing and claims practices.

Long-term insurance is still a viable option for many, although the number of insurers selling it has declined. Many insurers have sold off their long-term-care books of business in favor of other products as the market has become saturated. Before purchasing a policy, consumers should make sure that they understand exactly what's covered and what isn't. Avoid purchasing policies from insurers who do not have a solid financial background and check into how many complaints have been filed against them for nonpayment. All insurance companies are rated by agencies such as A.M Best, Standard & Poor and Moody's.

Read more:

http://law.freeadvice.com/insurance_law/long_term_care/history-of-long-term-care.htm#ixzz44172ntCU

THE CHANGING FACE OF LONG-TERM-CARE POLICIES

From premium costs to qualifying criteria, long-term-care insurance policies are changing. Whether you own a policy or are shopping for one, here are some factors to consider:

- **Increasing premiums.** When you purchase a policy, your premium isn't fixed. While annual premium increases are to be expected, some insurance vendors have recently requested increases as high as 85-95 percent. The reason? Many insurance providers didn't predict the dramatically rising costs of health care or the declining interest rate environment.

- **Changing qualifications.** Because of the financial instability faced by long-term-care insurance providers, insurance is increasingly being sold to clients who present less of a liability. Prospective policyholders are now being turned down for relatively common health conditions, such as arthritis and diabetes. And in order to qualify for benefit payouts, clients must require assistance with at least two of the following activities: bathing, dressing, eating, maintaining continence, toileting and transferring from bed to chair.

- **The "crystal ball" factor.** While clients were once able to purchase unlimited lifetime benefits, policies now restrict purchasers to a fixed time period and payout amount. As a result, clients are forced to guess how much coverage they'll need— and often wind up overpaying for coverage they don't use, or underestimating and falling short financially. Because long-term-care insurance purchases are made well in advance of when clients actually need the benefits, policy selection often boils down to a guess.

THE RISE OF THE HYBRID POLICY

In response to increasingly pricey and exclusionary traditional long-term-care insurance, hybrid policies are growing in popularity. For example, certain life insurance policies—many of which promise no rate increases for the duration of the contract—allow benefits to be applied to long-term-care costs if needed. Or single-premium modified endowments allow clients to ensure care for a predetermined period of time in exchange for a lump-sum payment, eliminating the risk of premium hikes. Some providers even offer returns on the unused benefits if the policy is canceled.

With the growing availability of more flexible and accessible insurance policies, traditional long-term-care insurance is no longer a one-size-fits-all solution. Choosing the best insurance policy for your situation can have significant financial benefits over time. Because policy details can be confusing, it's wise to consult a financial advisor prior to purchase. When selected carefully, long-term-care insurance can deliver peace of mind and ensure your comfort later in life. And while it may seem as though the need for benefits is a long way off, it's best to plan as early as possible.

WHAT'S YOUR LIFE EXPECTANCY?

You may have a longer life expectancy than you realize. A male Boomer who has just turned sixty-five can expect to live another 18.6 years. A Boomer woman who is the same age has an even longer life expectancy: an additional 20.9 years. That means that if people retire the day they turn sixty-five, they should have retirement savings that will support them for another eighteen to twenty years.

Here's another way to look at life expectancy. According to USAA, if you're part of a married sixty-five-year-old couple, there's a:

- 92 percent chance at least one of you will live to age eighty.

- 57 percent chance one of you will live to age ninety.

- 11 percent chance one of you will live to age one hundred.

Are you prepared to live to age one hundred? Many people aren't. Yet there's a good chance that you'll exceed your life expectancy. If that happens, you need savings that will support you as you grow older.

Not only are people tending to live longer in retirement, but they may also face far more health care expenses than they realize. A sixty-five-year-old couple who retired in 2012 will need $240,000 just to pay for medical expenses, according to Fidelity. And that estimate doesn't include the cost of over-the-counter medications, dental care, and long-term care.

Aging Baby Boomers may also face other challenges, such as difficulty finding doctors who accept new Medicare patients. Other possible changes to a stressed Medicare system include means-testing, an increased eligibility age, and waiting periods.

So, what should Baby Boomers who are nearing retirement do to help reduce the risk of running out of money? One step you can take is to get a better sense of your own life expectancy. There are numerous online calculators that will help you do this. You simply enter some of your personal information (such as your family history, age, and current health conditions) and then get a personalized estimate of how long you may live.

Once you have a better idea of how long you may live, you can adapt your retirement planning to that expectation. You may end up saving more aggressively for retirement, adjusting your portfolio allocation because of a new investment time frame, or cutting your living expenses so that you can reduce portfolio withdrawals. Your life expectancy and anticipated health problems may also affect your decision about whether or not to purchase long-term-care insurance.

Having a better sense of your life expectancy can also affect decisions about when to start taking

Social Security benefits. If your life expectancy is lower than average, you may benefit from starting to collect benefits sooner. But if you expect to live a long time, you may want to put off claiming for as long as possible, so that you can get a higher monthly check once you do start drawing benefits.

It wasn't all that long ago a family was only three generations deep—grandparent, parent, and child. But as life expectancies increase, four generations are common, and five generations are no longer unheard of. The financial impact of this demographic change has been dramatic. Instead of a family focused only on its own finances, it may have to deal with financial issues that cross generations. Here is a sampling of some multi-generational financial issues.

- **Aging parents.** Where once people lived only a few years into retirement, now they live fifteen, twenty, thirty years or more. If the parents can't take care of themselves, or they can't afford to pay for high-cost, long-term care, either at home or in a facility, their children may need to step forward. A geriatric care professional may be helpful here.

A host of financial issues is involved. One of the keys is to have a heart-to-heart, money-to-money talk about health-care issues, long-term-care needs ("What nursing home would you want to go to, Mom?") and how likely the aging parents can pay for them. Do they have assets to tap? Should their children buy long-term-care insurance for them? Or are their assets so few they will likely qualify for Medicaid assistance? What can the children realistically do for their parents without jeopardizing their own financial future?

- **Passing on the estate.** This is the opposite issue—grandparents who have more than enough financial resources to take care of themselves. The question is, what do they intend to do with their money? Will they pass it on to their children and grandchildren while they are still alive to make their heirs' lives easier, to see their gifts enjoyed, to teach their heirs how to use the assets and to ease a potential estate-tax problem? Or will they wait until death to pass on their estate? Will they spend as much of it as they can before they die? Or do they prefer to donate it to their favorite charities and force their heirs to make their own way in life? Answers to these questions have tremendous financial planning ramifications for the generations that follow.

- **Business succession.** Business owners need to decide well before they want to retire what they want to do with the family business. Do they want to sell it to outsiders or keep it in the family? Is anyone in the family willing and able to run it? Don't look down just one generation. Perhaps a grandchild is the best choice. What tax issues are involved? This is a complex, multi-generational issue that will require the services of financial professionals.

- **College versus retirement.** This is a multi-generational issue many families are familiar with. How do you provide children with advanced education while continuing to adequately save for your own retirement (and perhaps take care of aging parents)? The answer many financial planners give these days is to make your retirement the priority. Kids can find financial aid and work their way through college. You don't get financial aid for retirement.

  Here's where another generation can help, too. Grandparents, particularly grandparents who may face an estate tax issue, can directly pay their grandchild's tuition without the payments triggering a gift tax.

- **Loaning money.** It's not uncommon for parents to stake their children's first home or for grandparents to help a grandchild start a business. But family loans are fraught with potential family friction if the loans aren't paid back, and there are tax issues, as well. Do you bail out a financially struggling family member who doesn't deserve to be bailed out? What impact will the loan have on the lender's own financial goals, such as retirement?

These are only a smattering of the many multi-generational financial issues that may arise. The issues often are complicated by the fact that people don't like to talk about their money, and that different generations often view money and its use in different ways. That's why it's important to try to bring the generations together at a meeting to discuss interconnected issues. Consider bringing in financial professionals. They can explain complex issues in understandable terms, provide needed expertise with an independent viewpoint, and motivate action.

OTHER LONG-TERM-CARE INSURANCE CONSIDERATIONS

One of the biggest factors when preparing for retirement is health care insurance. People don't usually like to think about aging or possibly needing long-term health care. However, it's important that you do consider and make decisions on your long-term needs.

Long-term health care can be costly, so deciding whether to insure yourself is an important one. Long-term health care means care needed over a period of time because of a chronic illness or disability. The kind of care needed can range from simple help in your home to skilled care in a nursing home or hospital. To cover these costs, some individuals decide to purchase long-term-care insurance. So what do you need to know before you commit?

There are a few basic considerations before you decide whether to buy a long-term-care policy.

- **Premiums and Your Income.** Premiums increase over time—and since your income is likely to decrease during retirement, you will need to factor today's costs and future costs of keeping the policy active. The cost is around $3,000 to $6,000 per year. Rates for long-term-care insurance are not guaranteed and usually increase 3 percent to 5 percent a year.

- **Age and Health.** If you decide on a policy, get it while you are younger and in good health—it costs less.

- **Taxes.** The benefits are not taxed as income, and you can deduct the premium cost from federal income taxes.

- **Family.** Determine whether you have a support system to provide help with your health care if needed. Review your family medical history regarding long-term care.

Long-term-care insurance is expensive; however, it can be money well-spent. It covers most costs for nursing homes, assisted-living facilities and home health care. The likelihood of needing long-term care at some point in your life is high—government research shows 70 percent of people sixty-five or older will need such care. However, because of advanced medical care and healthier living, the average stay in a nursing home has become shorter— meaning less cost.

If you do decide to buy a policy, review the different coverage options. Since future care is unpredictable, a policy with flexible options should be considered.

CHAPTER 10

How to Hire a Fiduciary to Manage the Care

Sons or daughters are often appointed by courts to serve as their parent's conservator or guardian. In fact, laws are designed to promote family members to these positions. If that happens to you, here is my confidential insider scoop: if you have the luxury, hire someone to serve as professional fiduciary. You won't regret it.

What many eldercare caregivers and caretakers do not realize is the true role of a fiduciary. Fiduciaries are appointed as a conservator of the entire person, not just their assets. Fiduciaries are responsible for the care, housing, and the freedom of an impaired individual who is adjudicated to be a danger to himself or others, or cannot manage his or her affairs.

Legally, What are You Getting Yourself Into?

Caregivers and caretakers need to learn a whole new vocabulary of words like fiduciary, conservator, and adjudicate. A conservator is a protector, custodian, or guardian of a person. The definition of "adjudicate" is the act of making a judgment regarding a person or about a situation, most often in a courtroom. An example of adjudication is the judges on the Supreme Court issuing a ruling on whether a law is Constitutional. In eldercare, a judge can adjudicate whether a person is mentally and physically fit to manage his or her own affairs.

Some caregivers and caretakers mistakenly focus on just the fiduciary's financial role—being responsible for managing assets and handling investments for trusts, conservatorships, and estates. But it is not all about the money. He or she is appointed by an individual or court to assume a position of trust and responsibility. As a trustee, a professional fiduciary is responsible for carrying out the terms of the trust. As a conservator, the fiduciary is responsible for managing the estate and personal affairs of an individual who had been legally determined to be physically or mentally incapacitated.

As a reminder, the legal definition of a fiduciary is a person who has the power and obligation to act for another (often called the beneficiary) under circumstances which require total trust, good faith, and honesty. The most common is a trustee of a trust. Fiduciaries can include business advisers, attorneys, guardians, administrators of estates, real estate agents, bankers, stockbrokers, title companies, or anyone who undertakes to assist someone who places complete confidence and trust in them.

According to law.com, characteristically the fiduciary has greater knowledge and expertise about the matters being handled. A fiduciary is legally held to a standard of conduct and trust above that of a stranger or of a casual business person. The fiduciary must avoid *self-dealing or conflicts of interest* (a huge problem in some families, unfortunately) in which the potential benefit to the fiduciary is in conflict with what is best for the person.

For example, an investment advisor must consider the best investment for the client and not buy or sell on the basis of what brings the highest commission, as that would be self-dealing. While a fiduciary and the beneficiary may join together in a business venture or a purchase of property, the best interest of the beneficiary must be primary; absolute candor is required of the fiduciary. The person is trusting the fiduciary with their entire life.

ROLE OF ELDERCARE FIDUCIARY

Looking at the elderly person's complete health, well-being, and financial picture is the only way to properly assess sound financial advice. This encompasses everything: personal and business financial goals, along with their emotional well-being and personal objectives.

When an elderly person works with an estate planning attorney, they have the opportunity to name who they want as fiduciary. Ideally, the person selected will have the experience to foresee to the person's future financial and physical needs.

The median age of a professional fiduciary in California is fifty-eight, similar to financial planners, who have a median age of fifty-seven. In my opinion, being a fiduciary is too much to ask of most thirty-year-olds. There are just too many moving parts, and the wisdom gained from years of experience are a big asset. Fiduciaries are not there to handle a crisis; that is the role of first responders, such as paramedics and police officers. The fiduciary is there to take measured, thoughtful actions on behalf of the person's physical well-being and financial assets.

THE FIDUCIARY YOU DO NOT GET TO SELECT

But there is a situation when an elderly person does not get to select their own fiduciary. This occurs when an elderly person is adjudicated to not have the capacity to handle his or her own affairs and/or is a danger to self and/or others. In this situation, a judge in a court of law (generally called a probate court) appoints someone to manage and control the person's property and/or to act on his or her behalf. Some states call this special fiduciary a guardian; in others states, they are known as conservators.

As we live in a collection of 50 states, we have 50 different state laws that control how and when a guardian or conservator can be appointed. In general, a guardian or conservator is appointed in the following way: Someone, such as a family member, friend, or a government worker (for example, a social worker working with Adult Protective Services or some other agency that deals with mental health, children, and others with developmental disabilities) files an action in a probate court (or the court of competent jurisdiction) to have someone placed under conservatorship or guardianship. Both the person who needs to be conserved and the person bringing the legal action are represented by attorneys.

A probate judge then hears the case, witnesses and experts give testimony, and the person who is being sued for guardianship is also heard. The judge then makes a decision about whether or not to place the person under the court's supervision, and, if necessary, names a fiduciary to manage affairs and/ or to make living and health care decisions for the ward (the person needing to be conserved or placed under guardianship). State laws define a lack of capacity to handle one's affairs differently than having competency, so you will need to read more about your own state's laws and the laws of your family member's state of residency as to how all of this works. No two states are alike.

Even with good estate planning, naming an agent under a power of attorney document and/or trustee of a living trust, a guardian, or a conservator may still be necessary. In situations involving large estates, there have been many instances when a perfectly competent person may have wanted to be placed under guardianship or conservatorship.

At my practice, we have heard of public fights in the courts here in the U.S. and in other countries where very rich persons have someone exerting undue influence on them in business matters (where we are talking about Fortune 500 or similar companies). The adult may not be able to make complex decisions because of someone's outside influence, or because they are too emotionally involved to be objective as a director of a publicly held corporation (who also has a fiduciary duty to the shareholders). Other examples of undue influence can come from clergy, cults, criminals, family members, and abusers.

Another situation that may require guardianship or conservatorship is in the case of severe mental illness that causes a person to be a danger to themselves or others. Remember, earlier I said that agents under durable power of attorneys, trustees under living trusts, and others like these can be hired or fired at will. Sometimes, guardianship proceedings are brought to undo changes made to a will, trust, or other business decisions that could have been made under duress or are a detriment to the individual's estate or to his person.

As you can now see, guardianship and conservatorships are very public, and they can be embarrassing and expensive. Good estate planning can reduce the need for guardianship and conservatorships. As you can also see, however, there are situations when the need for a guardianship or conservatorship is unavoidable. Many estate planning attorneys recommend that you name someone to act as your guardian or conservator in your durable power of attorney documents, so at least you will have made some indication to the judge in the probate court as to whom you would like to serve in this special position.

CHOOSE OR HAVE SOMEONE ELSE CHOOSE

What many people do not realize is this: if they don't take action to help a family member, then somebody else is going to do it, and it may not be the person they want. If family members are so bad that a court has to intervene, then there are some serious problems going on. Rare are the times when a medical situation will cause an emergency guardianship. In my experience, a guardian is typically needed because a person is getting progressively worse and worse, and the family shows total apathy and does not intervene.

When that happens, then the court steps in. A judge will often appoint a professional fiduciary who is worthy of the role and proven to be competent. If you as caregiver or caretaker need to appoint a fiduciary, then you should select a professional like the court does. Don't go with just anybody; find out who the court appoints. Why would you want to select someone a court would not appoint as a fiduciary?

Selecting a professional fiduciary in advance of when you need them is a good idea, and you need to empower them for when the time comes for them to assume the role. The time to select is when the estate planning attorney draws up the estate planning documents.

Here is how to screen a professional fiduciary.

- **First, check the background and experience of the fiduciary to see if it is related to what is needed.** This is the finances part of the equation. Does the elderly person have real property? Oil wells? A small business? A farm? Paper assets like stocks and bonds? Do they have intellectual property? Then research fiduciaries with experience with those types of assets. Remember that different situations require different expertise.

- **Secondly, consider the elderly person's physical needs.** This is the physical part of the equation.

Do they have diabetes? Parkinson's? Alzheimer's? Some other chronic disease? Have they had a stroke? A heart bypass? A fiduciary with experience with helping people who have a particular chronic disease or health will know about resources and services that are available. Do they have physical challenges? Will the fiduciary be able to find them handymen, plumbers, and people who repair things? Is this the kind of person who could help find a plumber for them at 2 a.m. when a pipe bursts? Or, God forbid, a bail bondsman in the middle of the night for a DUI? These things must be considered. Again, different situations require different types of experts.

What does the court look for? The court considers the person's financial and physical situation and then looks for a fiduciary with the best match of experience. And so should you.

MANAGE, BUT NOT MANUFACTURE

Fiduciaries manage people and portfolios, but they don't manufacture or create home health care agencies or financial portfolios. The fiduciary may have to handle or liquidate portfolios, but they do not create portfolios. Fiduciaries may have to manage caregivers, such as home health care nurses or friendly neighbors, but they do not give the care. While nurses and social workers provide care, the job of the fiduciary is to oversee the care. The fiduciary is like the general contractor on a construction project who manages all the subcontractors, such as carpenters, electricians, and painters. Likewise, fiduciaries work with lawyers, nurses, and social workers in order to piece together a custom care plan. Total care plans are not something you can buy off the rack, but must be tailored to the individual.

A metaphor I often use to explain the relationship is drawn from the military chain of command. The fiduciary is a junior officer in the military—like a major in an army or a lieutenant commander in a navy. A junior officer can only carry out orders, but cannot change orders given by a commanding officer. The junior officer is given battlefield discretion in how best to carry out the orders. They are expected to use their best judgment to make numerous decisions in the field.

For a fiduciary junior officer, the commanding officer is the trust document or laws of the state. The fiduciary has discretion in how to carry out the orders but cannot change the order. An executor in a will is a fiduciary and has some discretion in how to carry out the wishes of the deceased. But the executor does not have the power to change what the diseased wanted to be done; only a court or an alive and competent person revising their own will can change the orders.

There are checks and balances to manage a fiduciary. For instance, a fiduciary must report such items as income and expenses to the courts or to the beneficiaries.

A final confidential piece of advice: not all fiduciaries are created equal, so choose wisely.

Appendix

Acknowledgments

The author wishes to thank the following people for helping to make this book happen: my editor Henry DeVries, who helped me find my voice in written words, my daughter Jacquelyn, who will have the role of fiduciary for her parents, and to Ellie Page, a professional fiduciary who showed me the ropes, shared the difficulties, her vision, and her passion to act in the best interest of another.

Resources

Tips on Improving Patient-Practitioner Communication

www.healthinaging.org/resources

Good communication between you and your health care practitioners—the physicians, nurse practitioners, nurses, physician assistants and other health care professionals you see—is essential to good care.

Living with Multiple Health Problems

www.healthinaging.org/resources

More than half of all adults sixty-five and older have three or more chronic (ongoing) medical problems, such as heart disease, diabetes, cancer, or arthritis. Caring for older patients with multiple health problems can be tricky, even for health care professionals who specialize in caring for older people. For example, prescribing medications for a patient with multiple health problems is more difficult than when the patient has one health problem. A drug may be useful in treating one of the patient's health problems, but it might make another worse.

Medicare Rights Center (MRC)

www.medicarerights.org

A national consumer service organization dedicated to ensuring that older adults and people with disabilities get good, affordable health care. MRC's website contains information about Medicare benefits, options and changes, examples of interesting cases they have dealt with, and resources for getting involved in their consumer advocacy work. Additionally, they have updated information for consumers about the upcoming changes in Medicare and how they will affect their health coverage.

Aging Parents and Elder Care

www.aging-parents-and-elder-care.com

Articles, comprehensive checklists, and links to key resources designed to make it easier for family caregivers to quickly find the information they need and avoid overlooking something important in the care of their loved one.

Nursing Home Abuse Resource

www.nursing-home-abuse-resource.com

Learn about ways to prevent, detect, and report nursing home abuse. Contact a nursing home abuse lawyer to learn your legal rights.

Agency for Health Care Policy and Aging

www.ahcpr.gov

Agency for Healthcare Research and Quality (AHRQ), formerly the Agency for Health Care Policy and Research. Practical health care information, research findings, and data to help consumers, health providers, health insurers, researchers, and policymakers make informed decisions about health care issues.

The Alzheimer's Association

www.alz.org

The Alzheimer's Association, a national network of chapters, is the largest national voluntary health organization committed to finding a cure for Alzheimer's and helping those affected by the disease.

ALZHEIMERS.COM

www.alzheimers.com

Alzheimers.com is dedicated to preventing and treating the cognitive decline of Alzheimer's disease, and to providing practical, up-to-the-minute information to empower Alzheimer's caregivers to manage the disease more confidently, effectively, and economically.

THE NATIONAL ACADEMY OF ELDER LAW ATTORNEYS

www.naela.org

The National Academy of Elder Law Attorneys, Inc. is a nonprofit association that assists lawyers, bar organizations and others who work with older clients and their families. Established in 1987, the Academy provides a resource of information, education, networking and assistance to those who must deal with the many specialized issues involved with legal services to the elderly and disabled.

Center for Long-Term-Care Financing

www.centerltc.com

The Center for Long-Term Care Reform is a private institute dedicated to ensuring quality long-term care for all Americans by promoting public policy that targets scarce public resources to the neediest, while encouraging people who are young, healthy, and affluent enough, to take responsibility for themselves.

The internet Drug Index

www.rxlist.com

A directory of brand name and generic drugs and their side effects.

Consumer Information About Physical Therapy and The Aging Adult

http://geriatricspt.org

Exercises and information on caring for older adults.

U.S. Government Site for Consumer Health and Human Services

www.healthfinder.gov

For consumer health and human services information. A service of the U.S. Department of Health and Human Services.

Planning for Eldercare Homepage

www.longtermcarelink.net/ncpc.htm

Contained here are thirty-four in-depth chapters, totaling over 690 printable pages, from nine experts and covering all areas of long-term-care planning, or as it's more commonly called, eldercare planning.

LegalAce.com

www.legalace.com

Having a will is one of the best ways to protect your family. Make legal wills online inexpensively and fast.

About the Author

Chris Cooper is a passionate advocate for people trying to meet the often crushing costs of medical care. He found his passion early on, while working in nursing homes and hospitals. After completing paramedic training and obtaining a nursing degree, he pursued his interest in how people could finance health care, primarily acute care. He realized that chronic long-term care leads to financial devastation for many people, especially retirees.

Chris is a professional fiduciary licensed in California. As a professional fiduciary, Chris works with seniors, disabled individuals and others who can't manage their affairs on their own. He assists them with everything from day-to-day financial issues to investment and estate management. Chris is also the founder of Eldercare Advocates, which provides geriatric care management and long-term-care consulting.

Chris has established fee-only financial planning practices in Toledo, Ohio, and San Diego, California. In addition to the highly respected Certified Financial Planner designation, he has a Master of Science in financial services with a specialization in financial planning. Other career accomplishments include designations as a Chartered Life Underwriter and Chartered Financial Consultant, admission to the prestigious Registry of Financial Planning Practitioners, and a graduate certificate in gerontology. He is enrolled to practice and represent clients before the Internal Revenue Service. He also represents clients in fair hearing processes before the Department of Health and Human Services at the state level.

Chris has appeared on CNBC Power Lunch, NBC Today, and CBS Morning Show. Chris is regularly quoted in The Wall Street Journal, and other newspapers and magazines nationwide.

Index